smart CHOICE
2nd Edition

Success – Every day, on every page

Ken Wilson

OXFORD UNIVERSITY PRESS

OXFORD
UNIVERSITY PRESS

198 Madison Avenue
New York, NY 10016 USA

Great Clarendon Street, Oxford OX2 6DP UK

Oxford University Press is a department of the University of Oxford. It furthers the University's objective of excellence in research, scholarship, and education by publishing worldwide in

Oxford New York

Auckland Cape Town Dar es Salaam Hong Kong Karachi Kuala Lumpur Madrid Melbourne Mexico City Nairobi New Delhi Shanghai Taipei Toronto

With offices in

Argentina Austria Brazil Chile Czech Republic France Greece Guatemala Hungary Italy Japan Poland Portugal Singapore South Korea Switzerland Thailand Turkey Ukraine Vietnam

OXFORD and OXFORD ENGLISH are registered trademarks of Oxford University Press in certain countries.

© Oxford University Press 2011

Database right Oxford University Press (maker)

No unauthorized photocopying

All rights reserved. No part of this publication may be reproduced, stored in a retrieval system, or transmitted, in any form or by any means, without the prior permission in writing of Oxford University Press, or as expressly permitted by law, or under terms agreed with the appropriate copyright clearance organization. Enquiries concerning reproduction outside the scope of the above should be sent to the ELT Rights Department, Oxford University Press, at the address above.

You must not circulate this book in any other binding or cover and you must impose this same condition on any acquirer.

Any websites referred to in this publication are in the public domain and their addresses are provided by Oxford University Press for information only. Oxford University Press disclaims any responsibility for the content.

General Manager: Laura Pearson
Editorial Director, International Schools and Adult: Pam Murphy
Executive Publishing Manager: Erik Gundersen
Managing Editor: Chris Newton
Development Editor: Hannah Ryu
Director, ADP: Susan Sanguily
Executive Design Manager: Maj-Britt Hagsted
Associate Design Manager: Michael Steinhofer
Electronic Production Manager: Julie Armstrong
Cover Design: Molly Scanlon
Image Manager: Trisha Masterson
Production Coordinator: Elizabeth Matsumoto
Senior Manufacturing Controller: Eve Wong

ISBN: 978-0-19-440705-2 Student Book (pack component)
ISBN: 978-0-19-440737-3 Student Book (pack)
ISBN: 978-0-19-440733-5 Access card (pack component)
ISBN: 978-0-19-440725-0 Online practice (pack component)

Printed in China

This book is printed on paper from certified and well-managed sources

10 9 8

ACKNOWLEDGMENTS

Cover photos a montage of the following:

Jurgen Ziewe/Shutterstock.com; oriontrail/Shutterstock.com; sl2007/Shutterstock.com; Olga Miltsova/Shutterstock.com; Stakhiv Arsen Ivanovich/Shutterstock.com; ssuaphotos/Shutterstock.com; emin kuliyev/Shutterstock.com; vovan/Shutterstock.com; Vladitto/Shutterstock.com; urosr/Shutterstock.com; nadiya_sergey/Shutterstock.com; Olga Sapegina/Shutterstock.com; Maridav/Shutterstock.com; Tom Fullum/istockphoto.com; Maridav/istockphoto.com; Rüstem GÜRLER/iStockphoto.com (Imac), inside back cover.

Illustrations by:

Barb Bastian: 43, 83; Kathy Baxendale: 26, 75; Vanessa Bell/NB Illustration: 46, 47(t), 90, 102; Patrick Boyer/illustrationweb.com: 15, 53, 89, 101; Harry Briggs: 58, 67(t); Claudia Carlson: 63; Grace Chen Design & Illustrations: 55; Kun-Sung Chung Illustration: 16; Monica Laita/AA Reps Inc.: 13, 85, 97; Karen Minot: 29, 56, 80 (map), 113; Marc Mones/AA Reps Inc.: 2, 88, 100; Greg Paprocki: 44(t), 82; Geo Parkin/AA Reps Inc: 9, 19(t)(b), 21, 34, 39(b), 44(b), 67(b), 70; Leif Peng: 33(b), 36; Gavin Reece/New Division: 30, 42; Robert Schuster: 47(b); Ben Shannon: 64, 76; Lucy Truman/New Division 22, 24, 50, 62; Glenn Urieta: 39(t); Graham White: 93, 105; Michael Steinhofer/OUP, piii (mp3 player)

We would also like to thank the following for permission to reproduce the following photographs:

Stephen Ogilvy, pg. 3 (teacher); pg. 3 (teacher); pg. 3 (teacher); Photodisc, pg. 3 (strawberry); Location photography by Mannicmedia, pg. 4 (video); Mark Leibowitz / Masterfile, pg. 5 (couple taking self-portrait); Image Source / Alamy, pg. 5 (Asian male friends); James Darell / Getty Images, pg. 5 (woman with red hair); Location photography by Mannicmedia, pg. 6 (video); Dominique Charriau / WireImage / Getty Images, pg. 8 (DiCaprio); Merie W. Wallace / 20th Century Fox / Paramount / The Kobal Collection, pg. 8 (Titanic); Michael Mahovlich / Masterfile, pg. 10 (pilot); Andersen Ross / Digital Vision / Getty Images, pg. 10 (doctor); Jose Luis Pelaez Inc / Blend Images / Getty images, pg. 10 (architect); Terry Vine / Blend Images / Alamy, pg. 10 (teacher); Mike Powell / Getty images, pg. 10 (goalie); George D. Sota / Masterfile, pg. 10 (singer); George De Sota / Getty Images, pg. 10 (fashion model); Paul Doyle / Alamy, pg. 10 (actor); Ken Fisher / Getty Images, pg. 10 (policewoman); V Stock / Alamy, pg. 10 (taxi driver); Location photography by Mannicmedia, pg. 11 (video); Asia Images Group / Getty Images, pg. 11 (student holding a book); Bill Schildge / Pacific Stock, pg. 14 (zookeeper); SuperStock / SuperStock, pg. 14 (tiger); Stephen Ogilvy, pg. 14 (window washer); Antony Nettle / Alamy, pg. 14 (Swiss Re Tower); Paul Simcock / Photodisc / Getty Images, pg. 16 (African American man); Location photography by Mannicmedia, pg. 17 (video); Photodisc, pg. 18 (Chuck); George Doyle / Stockbyte / Getty Images, pg. 18 (Dora); Taesam Do / Foodpix / Getty Images, pg. 20 (kimchi); Topic Photo Agency IN / AGE Fotostock, pg. 20 (Seoul); Asia Photopress / Alamy, pg. 20 (Pojangmacha); Jack Clark / The Image Works, pg. 20 (San Francisco); Jeff Greenberg / The Image Works, pg. 20 (breakfast plate); Christopher Elwell / ShutterStock, pg. 20 (pancakes); Frilet Patrick / AGE Fotostock, pg. 21 (diner); Frances M. Roberts / Alamy, pg. 21 (Chinese restaurant); Jeff Greenberg / The Image Works, pg. 21 (Mexican restaurant); Somos, pg. 23 (chef); Location photography by Mannicmedia, pg. 25 (video); MIXMA / Getty Images, pg. 25 (Asian woman smiling); Stockbyte / Getty Images, pg. 26 (woman stretching); Nick Dolding / Getty Images, pg. 27 (man with dreads); RubberBall / Imagetate, pg. 27 (bald man); Punchstock, pg. 27 (woman with floral shirt); Greg Nelson / Sports Illustrated / Getty Images, pg. 28 (Yao Ming); Jack Hollingsworth / Photdisc / Getty Images, pg. 30 (man smiling); Location photography by Mannicmedia, pg. 31 (video); Warner Bros. / Courtesy Everett Collection, pg. 31 (Harry Potter DVD); Glow Images / Getty Images, pg. 32 (men reading); Vincent Abbey / Photographer's Direct, pg. 35 (woman on cell phone); pg. 35 (woman on cell phone); pg. 35 (woman on cell phone); Location photography by Mannicmedia, pg. 37 (video); Kris Timken / Blend Images / Getty Images, pg. 37 (girl with white shirt); Chad Johnston / Masterfile, pg. 38 (sick woman); Stephen Ogilvy, pg. 40 (band); Romilly Lockyer / The Image Bank / Getty Images, pg. 41 (birthday party); Martyn Chillmaid, pg. 41 (couple at café); Kazuhori Nogi / AFP / Getty Images, pg. 41 (people praying); British Retail Photography / Alamy, pg. 43 (café); Pedro Tavares / ShutterStock, pg. 43 (clock); Pando Hall / Photographer's Choice RF / Getty Images, pg. 44 (boy with glasses); Location photography by Mannicmedia, pg. 45 (video); Fuse / Getty Images, pg. 46 (woman trying on jeans); Stockbyte / Getty Images, pg. 48 (man with shopping bags); Robert Fried / Alamy, pg. 49 (Mexican woman); DAJ / Amana Images Inc., pg. 49 (Japanese students); Location photography by Mannicmedia, pg. 51 (video); Asia Images Group / Getty Images, pg. 51 (student holding a book); Jan Greune / Look / Getty Images, pg. 54 (two male friends); Yurok / Shutterstock, pg. 54 (two female friends); Andersen Ross / Blend Images / Getty Images, pg. 56 (girl with notebooks); Location photography by Mannicmedia, pg. 57 (video); Gail Mooney / Masterfile, pg. 59 (Statue of Liberty); Jeremy Woodhouse / Masterfile, pg. 59 (Copacabana); AGE Fotostock / SuperStock, pg. 59 (Notre Dame); Radek Smrcka / Shutterstock, pg. 60 (Colosseum); Alberto Biscaro / Mastefile, pg. 60 (St. Peter's Basilica); Angelo Cavalli / Photolibrary, pg. 60 (Roman Forum) R. Ian Lloyd / Masterfile, pg. 61 (mountains); AGE Fotostock / SuperStock, pg. 61 (mountain climber); Allstair Rennie / Shutterstock, pg. 61 (beach); Jeremy Woodhouse / Masterfile, pg. 61 (bird watcher); Ingram, pg. 61 (kiwi); LeggNet / iStockphoto, pg. 63 (Oscar); image 100, pg. 63 (Brigit); Photo Talk / iStockphoto, pg. 63 (Su-hyun); Location photography by Mannicmedia, pg. 65 (video); Paul Simcock / Photodisc / Getty Images, pg. 65 (African America man); AGE Fotostock / SuperStock, pg. 68 (Brian); Robert Mort / Getty Images, pg. 68 (Sydney harbor); Rob Reichenfeld / Dorling Kindersley / Getty Images, pg. 68 (Sydney Chinatown); J.A. Kraulis / Masterfile, pg. 68 (Vancouver); McCanner / Alamy, pg. 68 (Yaletown, Vancouver); Wei Yan / Masterfile, pg. 68 (Sarah); Phase4Photography / Shutterstock, pg. 69 (woman shopping); Hola Images / Getty Images, pg. 69 (girl eating junk food); Digital Vision / AGE Fotostock, pg. 69 (boy with headphones); Asia Images Group / Getty Images, pg. 70 (boy in denim jacket); Location photography by Mannicmedia, pg. 71 (video); Erkki & Hanna / Shutterstock, pg. 73 (Acapulco); Travelpix Ltd / Getty Images, pg. 73 (Rome); Ron Stroud / Masterfile, pg. 73 (Hong Kong); AGE Fotostock / Superstock, pg. 74 (ice hotel exterior); Andia / Alma, pg. 74 (ice hotel interior); Buena Vista Images / Digital Vision / Getty Images, pg. 74 (ice cube); Location photography by Mannicmedia, pg. 77 (video); MIXMA / Getty Images, pg. 77 (Asian woman smiling); Henry Westhein Photography / Alamy, pg. 78 (high-speed train); Ilja Masik / Shutterstock, pg. 79 (New York City); Melinda Fawver / Shutterstock, pg. 79 (Appalachians); Andy Z. / Shutterstock, pg. 79 (Hawaii); Torsten Blackwood / AFP / Getty Images, pg. 80 (solar-powered car); David R. Frazier Photolibrary, Inc. / Alamy, pg. 81 (commuter bus); PCL / Alamy, pg. 81 (subway); RedChopsticks / Getty Images, pg. 81 (people on bicycles); Denisenko Artem / Shutterstock, pg. 81 (motorcycle rider); Phil James, pg. 83 (Jim Conway); Ebet Roberts / Redfems / Getty Images, pg. 83 (New Orleans jazz band); Chris Graythen / Getty Images News / Getty Images, pg. 83 (New Orleans food booth); Dave M. Benett / Getty Images Entertainment / Getty Images, pg. 84 (Bono); Karim Jaafar / Stringer / AFP / Getty Images, pg. 84 (Kaka); Jeffrey Mayer / Getty Images, pg. 84 (Aniston); Fernando Medina / NBAE / Getty Images, pg. 84 (Shaquille O'Neal); Olivier Laban-Mattei / Getty Images, pg. 84 (Yeoh); Francois G. Durand / Wireimage / Getty Images, pg. 84 (Carrey); Photodisc, pg. 86 (ice cream); pg. 86 (salad); Milan Radosavljevic / AGE Fotostock, pg. 86 (fish on plate); Brand X Pictures / Getty Images, pg. 86 (cheese); Stockbyte / Getty Images, pg. 86 (noodles in cup); pg. 86 (Lucy); Indexstock, pg. 86 (pizza); The Image Bank / Getty Images, pg. 86 (Joe); Robertstock, pg. 86 (Paolo); Tom Merton / Getty Images, pg. 86 (Tom and May); Jump Photography / Shutterstock, pg. 86 (chicken); Stockbyte, pg. 86 (onion); Punchstock, pg. 86 (french fries); pg. 86 (hamburger); Stefano Tiraboschi / Shutterstock, pg. 86 (vegetables); Cooddy / Shutterstock, pg. 86 (bowl of soup); Hemera, pg. 86 (sushi); Ingram, pg. 86 (bread); Przemysaw / Shutterstock, pg. 86 (bowl of rice); Hemera, pg. 86 (shrimp); Ray Laskowitz / Superstock, pg. 87 (Amy); Mark Antman / The Image Works, pg. 87 (Chris); Orange Line Media / Shutterstock, pg. 87 (Sara); Juanmonino / iStock, pg. 87 (Gabriel); Monkey Business Images / Shutterstock, pg. 87 (Kim and Max); Digital Vision, pg 91 (two Asian girls); Jaume Gual / AGE Fotostock, pg. 91 (two boys laughing); beyond foto / AGE Fotostock, pg. 91 (friends cooking); Mark Leibowitz / Masterfile, pg. 92 (Times Square, New Years Eve); Gloria H. Chomica / Masterfile, pg. 92 (chuckwagon race); Vince Cavataio / Pacific Stock, pg. 94 (man jetskiing); John Cancalosi / AGE Fotostock, pg. 92 (kangaroo); Dave Saunders / Getty Images, pg. 94 (Sydney harbor); Sri Maiava Rusden / Pacific Stock, pg. 94 (woman taking a picture); Jeff Greenberg / AGE Fotostock, pg. 94 (Mexican restaurant); Richard Cummins / SuperStock, pg. 94 (Hollywood Walk of Fame); Sri Maiava Rusden / The Image Bank, pg. 95 (Fernando); Paul Cowan / Shutterstock, pg. 95 (Seoul); AVAVA / Shutterstock, pg. 95 (Ya-ting); pg. 95 (Brian); Ricardo Garza / Shutterstock, pg. 95 (Monterrey); Juanmonion / iStockphoto, pg. 95 (Carla); Rehoboth Foto / Shutterstock, pg. 95 (Hanoi); Purestock / Getty Images, pg. 95 (Dino); Styve Reineck / Shutterstock, pg. 95 (Dubai); Vinicius Tupinamba / Shutterstock, pg. 95 (Salvador); Supri Shuarjoto / Shutterstock, pg. 95 (Amy); Tororo Reactio / Shutterstock, pg. 95 (Okinawa); Dave M. Benett / Getty Images Entertainment / Getty Images, pg. 96 (Bono); Karim Jaafar / Stringer / AFP / Getty Images, pg. 96 (Kaka); Jeffrey Mayer / Getty Images, pg. 96 (Aniston); Fernando Medina / NBAE / Getty Images, pg. 96 (Shaquille O'Neal); Olivier Laban-Mattei / Getty Images, pg. 96 (Yeoh); Francois G. Durand / Wireimage / Getty Images, pg. 96 (Carrey); Hemera, pg. 98 (sushi); Cooddy / Shutterstock, pg. 98 (bowl of soup); Punchstock, pg. 98 (hamburger); pg. 98 (french fries); Jump Photography / Shutterstock, pg. 98 (chicken); Przemysaw / Shutterstock, pg. 98 (bowl of rice); The Image Bank / Getty Images, pg. 98 (Joe); Stockbyte / Getty Images, pg. 98 (Lucy); pg. 98 (noodles in cup); Robertstock, pg. 86 (Paolo); Tom Merton / Getty Images, pg. 98 (Tom and May); Milan Radosavljevic / AGE Fotostock, pg. 98 (fish on plate); Stockbyte, pg. 98 (onion); Brand X Pictures / Getty Images, pg. 98 (cheese); Stefano Tiraboschi / Shutterstock, pg. 98 (vegetables); Photodisc, pg. 98 (salad); pg. 98 (ice cream); Hemera, pg. 98 (shrimp); Indexstock, pg. 98 (pizza); Ray Laskowitz / Superstock, pg. 99 (Amy); Mark Antman / The Image Works, pg. 99 (Chris); Orange Line Media / Shutterstock, pg. 99 (Sara); Juanmonino / iStock, pg. 99 (Gabriel); Monkey Business Images / Shutterstock, pg. 99 (Kim and Max); Digital Vision, pg. 103 (two Asian girls); Jaume Gual / AGE Fotostock, pg. 103 (two boys laughing); beyond foto / AGE Fotostock, pg. 103 (friends cooking); Mark Leibowitz / Masterfile, pg. 104 (Times Square, New Years Eve); Gloria H. Chomica / Masterfile, pg. 104 (chuckwagon race); Vince Cavataio / Pacific Stock, pg. 106 (man jetskiing); John Cancalosi / AGE Fotostock, pg. 106 (kangaroo); Dave Saunders / Getty Images, pg. 106 (Sydney harbor); Sri Maiava Rusden / Pacific Stock, pg. 106 (woman taking a picture); Jeff Greenberg / AGE Fotostock, pg. 106 (Mexican restaurant); Richard Cummins / SuperStock, pg. 106 (Hollywood Walk of Fame); Sri Maiava Rusden / The Image Bank, pg. 107 (Fernando); Paul Cowan / Shutterstock, pg. 107 (Seoul); AVAVA / Shutterstock, pg. 107 (Ya-ting); pg. 107 (Brian); Ricardo Garza / Shutterstock, pg. 107 (Monterrey); Juanmonion / iStockphoto, pg. 107 (Carla); Rehoboth Foto / Shutterstock, pg. 107 (Hanoi); Purestock / Getty Images, pg. 107 (Dino); Styve Reineck / Shutterstock, pg. 107 (Dubai); Vinicius Tupinamba / Shutterstock, pg. 107 (Salvador); Supri Shuarjoto / Shutterstock, pg. 107 (Amy); Tororo Reactio / Shutterstock, pg. 107 (Okinawa); Stockbyte / Getty Images, pg. 108 (student with books); White / Photolibrary, pg. 109 (women eating sushi); Marc Romanelli / Getty Images, pg. 110 (man typing on laptop); Antonio M / Getty Images, pg. 110 (woman typing on laptop); Livia Corona / Getty Images, pg. 111 (student walking with books); Claudia Adams / DanitaDelimont.com, pg. 112 (Bangkok); Robert Warren / Getty Images, pg. 113 (man on sofa with laptop)

New for Smart Choice!

Online Practice with Progress Reports

Use the access card on the inside back cover to log in at www.sconlinepractice.com.

Smart Choice Online Practice features 10 engaging self-study activities for each unit. These activities will improve your vocabulary, grammar, speaking, and listening skills.

Progress Reports for Students, Teachers, and Administrators provide easy-to-read performance charts at the Student, Class, and Institutional levels.

Student Book Video

All-new video dialogues and listening activities will help you learn and practice everyday conversations.

Audio Download Center

With the Audio Download Center you can download Student Book and Workbook audio onto your computer, mobile phone, or digital audio player for any time, anywhere listening practice.

iii

Scope and Sequence

Unit	Conversation	Vocabulary	Grammar & Pronunciation
0 Essential English Pages 2–3	Key phrases for classroom interaction and learning		
1 Nice to meet you! Pages 4–9 ONLINE PRACTICE	• Introducing yourself • CONVERSATION PLUS: A class survey on favorite English words • Smart Talk: Who's that? (p. 84, 96)	Greetings	• Grammar: The present tense of *be* • Pronunciation: Syllable stress
2 What do you do? Pages 10–15 ONLINE PRACTICE	• Talking about personal information • CONVERSATION PLUS: A class survey on jobs • Smart Talk: What do they do? (p. 85, 97)	Jobs	• Grammar: Common *wh-* questions • Pronunciation: Reduction of *do you*
3 Do you like spicy food? Pages 16–21 ONLINE PRACTICE	• Talking about likes and dislikes • CONVERSATION PLUS: A class survey on food • Smart Talk: Does he like fish? (p. 86, 98)	Food and drink	• Grammar: The simple present • Pronunciation: Question intonation
Review Units 1–3 Pages 22–23	Conversation: Two people meeting for the first time Reading: "City Spotlight: Meet New York's best new chef!"		
4 How often do you do yoga? Pages 24–29 ONLINE PRACTICE	• Talking about habits and routines • CONVERSATION PLUS: A class survey about sports and exercise • Smart Talk: How often? (p. 87, 99)	Sports and exercise	• Grammar: Frequency adverbs • Pronunciation: Final s sounds
5 What are you watching? Pages 30–35 ONLINE PRACTICE	• Describing everyday activities • CONVERSATION PLUS: A survey on cell phone manners • Smart Talk: What is he doing? (p. 88, 100)	Everyday activities	• Grammar: The present continuous • Pronunciation: Reduction of *what is* and *what are*
6 Where were you yesterday? Pages 36–41 ONLINE PRACTICE	• Talking about past events • CONVERSATION PLUS: A class survey on past activities • Smart Talk: Where were they? (p. 89, 101)	Problems	• Grammar: The past tense of *be* • Pronunciation: Reduction of t in *wasn't* and *weren't*
Review Units 4–6 Pages 42–43	Conversation: A friend making excuses to another Reading: "Early Birds"		

iv

Listening	Reading & Writing	Learning Tips	Learning Outcomes
• Listening 1: Introductions • Listening 2: Responses	• An article about Leonardo DiCaprio • Writing: An e-mail about yourself (p. 108)		• Make an introduction • Make statements and questions • Understand information questions • Understand short biographies
• Listening 1: People talking about jobs and where they live • LISTENING PLUS: A continuation of a conversation in Listening 1.	• An interview with a zookeeper and a window washer • Writing: A paragraph with personal information (p. 108)	• Conversation: Extending the conversation	• Talk about jobs • Use *wh-* questions • Understand short conversations about people • Understand job descriptions
• Listening 1: People ordering in restaurants • LISTENING PLUS: A continuation of conversations in Listening 1.	• An article on street food in Seoul and Sunday brunch in San Francisco • Writing: A letter about your favorite restaurant (p. 109)	• Vocabulary: Using flashcards	• Talk about likes and dislikes • Use the simple present • Understand restaurant orders • Understand short texts about eating out
• Listening 1: Interviews about exercise routines • LISTENING PLUS: A continuation of conversations in Listening 1.	• An article on NBA basketball players and their training • Writing: An e-mail about your typical weekend (p. 109)	• Conversation: Taking turns	• Talk about habits and routines • Use frequency adverbs • Understand conversations about activities • Understand short texts about cities
• Listening 1: Phone conversations about what people are doing right now • LISTENING PLUS: A continuation of a conversation in Listening 1	• An article on eight ways to have better cell phone manners • Writing: A paragraph about what you're doing right now (p. 110)	• Vocabulary: Verb collocations	• Describe people's actions • Use the present continuous • Understand conversations about daily activities • Understand short texts about manners
• Listening 1: People talking about why they were late • LISTENING PLUS: A continuation of a conversation in Listening 1	• An interview with a pop music group • Writing: A diary entry about your last English class (p. 110)	• Conversation: Getting clarification	• Talk about past events • Use the simple past of *be* • Understand conversations about problems • Understand short texts about the past and the present

Unit	Conversation	Vocabulary	Grammar & Pronunciation
7 Which one is cheaper? Pages 44–49 ONLINE PRACTICE	• Making comparisons • CONVERSATION PLUS: A survey on clothing • Smart Talk: Which one do you like? (p. 90, 102)	Clothing	• Grammar: Comparative adjectives • Pronunciation: Word stress in comparisons
8 What's she like? Pages 50–55 ONLINE PRACTICE	• Describing people • CONVERSATION PLUS: A personality quiz • Smart Talk: My best friend (p. 91, 103)	Appearance and personality	• Grammar: *Be like* and *look like* • Pronunciation: Linked sounds with *does* and *is*
9 What can you do there? Pages 56–61 ONLINE PRACTICE	• Talking about cities • CONVERSATION PLUS: A travel advertisement for a good place to visit • Smart Talk: Don't miss it! (p. 92, 104)	Local attractions	• Grammar: *Can* and *can't* • Pronunciation: Reduced and unreduced *can* and *can't*
Review Units 7–9 Pages 62–63	Conversation: A street interview Reading: "World of Contact"		
10 Is there a bank near here? Pages 64–69 ONLINE PRACTICE	• Talking about places • CONVERSATION PLUS: A survey and discussion on the best places in town • Smart Talk: Is there a bank? (p. 93, 105)	Places around town	• Grammar: *There is* and *there are* • Pronunciation: Word stress in compound nouns
11 Did you have a good time? Pages 70–75 ONLINE PRACTICE	• Talking about vacations • CONVERSATION PLUS: A survey and discussion about great vacations • Smart Talk: What did you do there? (p. 94, 106)	Vacation activities	• Grammar: The simple past • Pronunciation: Reduction of *did you*
12 I'm going to go by car. Pages 76–81 ONLINE PRACTICE	• Talking about future plans • CONVERSATION PLUS: A survey and discussion about travel plans • Smart Talk: Where are they going to go? (p. 95, 107)	Transportation	• Grammar: *Going to* + verb • Pronunciation: Reduction of *going to*
Review Units 10–12 Pages 82–83	Conversation: A student telling his teacher about his vacation plans Reading: "A week in the life of … Jim Conway, rock journalist"		

Smart Talk
 Pages 84–107

Writing
 Pages 108–113

Audio scripts
 Pages 114–122

Grammar Reference & Practice
 Pages 123–134

Vocabulary List
 Pages 135–136

Listening	Reading & Writing	Learning Tips	Learning Outcomes
• Listening 1: People shopping for clothes and shoes • LISTENING PLUS: A continuation of conversations in Listening 1	• An article about people who love expensive designer clothes • Writing: An e-mail about clothes (p. 111)	• Vocabulary: Creating a picture dictionary	• Talk about clothes • Use comparative adjectives • Understand conversations about shopping • Understand short comparative texts
• Listening 1: People describing themselves and others • LISTENING PLUS: A continuation of a conversation in Listening 1	• An article about best friends • Writing: A paragraph about your personality and appearance (p. 111)	• Conversation: Expressing emotion	• Describe appearance and personality • Use *be like* and *look like* • Understand conversations describing people • Understand short texts about friends
• Listening 1: People talking about things for visitors to do in their cities • LISTENING PLUS: A continuation of monologues in Listening 1	• Advice and information on sightseeing in Rome • Writing: An article about things for visitors to do in your town (p. 112)	• Vocabulary: Learning words in context	• Talk about tourist sites • Use *can* and *can't* • Understand conversations about city attractions • Understand short texts about famous cities

Listening	Reading & Writing	Learning Tips	Learning Outcomes
• Listening 1: People asking a hotel receptionist for suggestions • LISTENING PLUS: A continuation of conversations in Listening 1	• An article about areas to visit in Sydney and Vancouver • Writing: An e-mail about the street where you live (p. 112)	• Conversation: Confirming information	• Talk about places around town • Use *there is* and *there are* • Understand exchanges about tourism • Understand short texts about favorite places
• Listening 1: People talking about things that went wrong on vacation • LISTENING PLUS: A continuation of a conversation in Listening 1	• An article about an ice hotel in Canada • Writing: A paragraph about your best (or worst) vacation (p. 113)	• Vocabulary: Making word associations	• Talk about vacation activities • Use the simple past • Understand conversations about vacations • Understand short texts about a hotel
• Listening 1: People talking about environmentally friendly vacation and travel plans • LISTENING PLUS: A continuation of monologues in Listening 1	• A blog by travelers in Australia • Writing: An e-mail about your city (p. 113)	• Conversation: Giving more information	• Talk about future plans • Use *going to* + verb • Understand conversations about travel plans • Understand short texts about travel activities

Essential English

Vocabulary

 1 Listen and repeat.

1. How do you say _____ in English?
2. How do you spell _____?

3. How do you say this word?
4. What does _____ mean?

5. Excuse me, can you repeat that, please?
   I'm sorry, I don't understand.
   I'm sorry, can you speak more slowly?

2

Essential English • Unit 0

Conversation

 1 Complete the conversations with the phrases in the box. Then listen and check your answers.

> Can you repeat that? How do you pronounce this word?
> How do you spell that? What's this called in English?
> What does *delighted* mean?

1. A <u>How do you pronounce this word?</u>
   B Which one? This one?
   A Uh-huh. That one.
   B Favorite.

2. A _____
   B It means "very happy."

3. A _____
   B That? That's called a keychain.
   A Sorry. _____
   B Sure. Keychain.

4. A How do you say 🍎 in English?
   B Strawberry.
   A _____
   B Strawberry? S-T-R-A-W-B-E-R-R-Y.

 2 PAIR WORK. Practice the conversations with a partner.

| SPEAKING | GRAMMAR | LISTENING | READING |
| Introduction | The verb *be* | Information questions | Biography |

Nice to meet you!

 How do you greet someone?

Conversation

CD1 Track 4

1 Listen to the conversation. Then practice it with a partner.

Marco   Hi. My name's <u>Marco</u>. What's your name?
Kelly   Hi, <u>Marco</u>. My name's <u>Kelly</u>.
Marco   So, where are you from, <u>Kelly</u>?
Kelly   I'm from <u>Toronto</u>. How about you?
Marco   I'm from <u>San Diego, California</u>.

2 PAIR WORK. Practice the conversation again. Replace the underlined words with information about you.

Pronunciation—*Syllable stress*

CD1 Track 5

1 Listen. Notice the stressed and unstressed syllables. Underline the stressed syllable in each word.

1. <u>Mar</u>•co
2. To•ron•to
3. Me•xi•co
4. Ko•re•a
5. Ca•na•da
6. stu•dent

2 Listen again and repeat. Which words have the same syllable stress?

4

Nice to meet you! • Unit 1

Language Practice

Statements with be — Grammar Reference page 123

I'm a student.
You're from Mexico.
He's from Korea.
She's from Canada.
We're students.
They're from the US.

I am → I'm
you are → you're
he is → he's
she is → she's
we are → we're
they are → they're

Possessive adjectives
my
your
his
her
our
their

I'm not a teacher. I'm a student.
He isn't from Brazil. He's from the US.
They aren't teachers. They're students.

is not → isn't
are not → aren't

1 Complete the sentences.

1. "Hi. My name is Nelson da Silva. I ___'m___ a photographer. This is my wife. _____ name is Gloria. We _____ from São Paulo, Brazil."

2. "Hi. ___My___ name is Jae-won Park. This is my friend. _____ name is Kun-woo Lee. We _____ from Korea. He _____ from Seoul, and I'm from Busan."

3. "Hi. My name ___'s___ Sarah Kilbane. I _____ an English teacher. I'm from Toronto, Canada. But my parents _____ from Canada. They're from Ireland. _____ names are Paul and Maggie."

2 PAIR WORK. Tell your partner about yourself.

5

Nice to meet you! • Unit 1

Conversation

1 Complete the conversation. Then listen and check your answers.

| a. friend | b. How are you | c. Fine |

Kelly   Hey, Marco! 1 _____?
Marco   2 _____, thanks. And you?
Kelly   Good, thanks.
Marco   Who's that girl over there?
Kelly   Her? That's my friend, Emily. Would you like to meet her?
Marco   Yes, please!

Kelly   Hi, Emily, this is my 3 _____, Marco. Marco, this is Emily.
Marco   Nice to meet you, Emily.
Emily   Nice to meet you, too.

Now practice the conversation with a partner.

2 PAIR WORK. Practice the conversation again. Use the ideas below.

| How are things | Pretty good | classmate |
| How's it going | Not bad | brother |

3 PAIR WORK. Introduce your partner to another classmate.

A _____, this is my friend, _____.
_____, this is _____.
B Nice to meet you, _____.
C Nice to meet you, too.

6

Nice to meet you! • Unit 1

Language Practice

Questions with be — Grammar Reference page 123

Are you a student?	Yes, I am.	No, I'm not.
Is he a teacher?	Yes, he is.	No, he isn't.
Is she an artist?	Yes, she is.	No, she isn't.
Are you actors?	Yes, we are.	No, we aren't.
Are they doctors?	Yes, they are.	No, they aren't.

Who's that?
What's your name?
Where are you from?
How are you?
How old are you?

Who is → Who's
What is → What's

1 Match the questions and answers.

1. What are your names? _e_
2. How old is he? ___
3. Where are you from? ___
4. Who's that? ___
5. Is she your girlfriend? ___
6. How are you? ___

a. We're from Australia.
b. Not bad, thanks. And you?
c. No, she isn't. She's my sister.
d. That's my brother.
e. He's Eric, and I'm Nancy.
f. He's 21.

2 PAIR WORK. Complete the conversations. Then practice them with a partner.

1. A Hi, Jane! _How are you_?
   B Hey, Alex! I'm fine. _____?
   A I'm fine, too.
   B _____ guy over there?
   A _____ my brother.

2. A Hi, my name's Brian. _____?
   B I'm Nancy.
   A _____?
   B I'm from Canada. _____?
   A I'm from England.

3 PAIR WORK. Put the lines in the correct order. Then use information about you and practice the conversation with a partner.

A
___ Nice to meet you, too.
___ My name's _____.
_1_ Hi! Are you a student?
___ Yes, I am. What's your name?

B
_2_ Yes, I am. And you? Are you a student?
___ Nice to meet you, _____.
___ My name's _____. What's your name?

 **Who's that?**

Student A: Turn to page 84.
Student B: Turn to page 96.

7

Nice to meet you! • Unit 1

Listening

1 Listen and circle the sentence you hear.

1. a. What's your name?
   b. What's her name? *(circled)*

2. a. He's from the US.
   b. She's from the US.

3. a. Where's she from?
   b. Where's he from?

4. a. How are you?
   b. Who are you?

5. a. We're from Canada.
   b. They're from Canada.

6. a. Is he a teacher?
   b. Is she a teacher?

2 Listen and circle the correct response.

1. a. Fine, thanks. *(circled)*
   b. I'm a student.

2. a. My name is …
   b. His name is …

3. a. Thanks.
   b. Nice to meet you, too.

4. a. That's my friend.
   b. She's from Japan.

5. a. He's from Australia.
   b. She's from Australia.

6. a. Yes, we are.
   b. No, she isn't.

Reading

BEFORE YOU READ What do you know about Leonardo DiCaprio?

The actor Leonardo DiCaprio was born on November 11th, 1974 in Los Angeles, California. His father, George, is Italian-American. His mother, Irmelin, is from Germany. His most famous role is Jack Dawson in the movie *Titanic*. His favorite movie is *The Godfather*.

1 Read the text about Leonardo DiCaprio and answer the questions.

1. What does he do?
2. Where is he from?
3. When is his birthday?
4. How old is he?
5. Where is his mother from?
6. What's his favorite movie?

Writing
Turn to page 108

Nice to meet you! • Unit 1

Conversation PLUS —*Your favorite words*

1 What are your three favorite words in English? Write them in the chart. What do they mean in your language?

	English word	Translation
1.		
2.		
3.		

2 CLASS ACTIVITY. Compare your answers. Write your classmates' favorite words in the chart.

What's your favorite word in English?

My favorite word in English is rainbow.

Rainbow. That's a nice word. My favorite word is …

Useful Language
What does _____ mean?
How do you spell _____?
Really? That's my favorite word, too!

	Name	Favorite word	Translation
1.			
2.			
3.			
4.			
5.			
6.			
7.			
8.			

Now I can...

- **SPEAKING** ☑ make an introduction.
- **GRAMMAR** ☐ make statements and questions with *be*.
- **LISTENING** ☐ understand information questions.
- **READING** ☐ understand short biographies.

| SPEAKING
Personal information | GRAMMAR
Wh- questions | LISTENING
Personal information | READING
Jobs |

What do you do?

Warm UP What jobs begin with the letters S, M, A, R, T?

Vocabulary

1 Look at the people. What are their jobs? Write the correct letter.

a. architect f. pilot
b. singer   g. actor
c. doctor   h. teacher
d. model   i. police officer
e. taxi driver j. soccer player

1. Michael _f_
2. Emi

3. Laura
4. Jose
5. Kim
6. Becky

7. Chris
8. Johnny
9. Lisa
10. Tom

CD1 Track 12 Listen and check your answers.

ONLINE PRACTICE

2 Write the correct word.

1. CHATEER _teacher_
2. ORCOTD _____
3. LIPTO _____
4. GRINSE _____
5. XAIT VIERRD _____
6. ICACHRETT _____

3 PAIR WORK. Think of people you know. What are their jobs? Tell your partner.

My friend is a singer.

Really? My friend is a singer, too.

10

What do you do? • Unit 2

Conversation

 1 Complete the conversation. Then listen and check your answers.

> a. English teacher   b. singer   c. Chicago

Brian	So, where do you live?
Stacy	Well, I'm from New York, but I live in 1 .
Brian	Interesting. And what do you do?
Stacy	I'm an 2 . What about you?
Brian	I'm a doctor. I work in a hospital in Seattle.
Stacy	Really? My sister lives in Seattle.
Brian	What does she do?
Stacy	She's a 3 .
Brian	What's her name?
Stacy	Suzy Davis.
Brian	Suzy? I know her!
Stacy	Really? Small world!

Now practice the conversation with a partner.

 2 PAIR WORK. Practice the conversation again. Use the ideas below. Add your own ideas.

Hawaii	architect	model
Mexico City	actress	police officer
_____	_____	_____

EXTEND THE CONVERSATION
Ask follow-up questions to extend the conversation

My sister lives in Seattle.

What does she do?

Conversation TIP

11

What do you do? • Unit 2

Language Practice

CD1 Track 14

Wh- questions

Grammar Reference page 124

What **do** you **do**?	**I'm** an architect.
Where **do** you **live**?	I **live** in Rio.
What **does** she **do**?	**She's** a college student.
Where **does** she **go** to school?	She **goes** to NYU.
What **do** they **do**?	**They're** pilots.
Who **do** they **work** for?	They **work** for Korean Air.
Where **do** they **work**?	They **work** in an airport.

ONLINE PRACTICE

1 Match the questions and answers.

1. What do you do? _b_
2. Where do you live? ___
3. What does she do? ___
4. Where do they go to school? ___

a. She's an architect.
b. I'm an office worker.
c. In Tokyo.
d. They go to the University of Texas.

2 Complete the conversations.

1. A Where ___do___ you ___live___?
   B I _____ in Los Angeles.

2. A Where _____ he _____?
   B He _____ in Singapore.

3. A What _____ you _____?
   B _____ a college student.

4. A What _____ they _____?
   B _____ teachers.

3 PAIR WORK. Complete the chart. Ask and answer the questions with information about you.

		You	Your partner
1.	Where do you live?		
2.	What do you do?		
3.	Where do you go to school?		
4.	Where do you work?		

Pronunciation—*Reduction of* do you

CD1 Track 15

1 Listen. Notice the reduced sound of *do you*.

Unreduced	Reduced
1. What do you do?	Whadaya do?
2. What do you study?	Whadaya study?
3. Where do you live?	Wherdaya live?
4. Where do you go?	Wherdaya go?

2 Listen again and repeat. Be sure to say the reduced sound.

12

Listening

BEFORE YOU LISTEN Look at the people. Where do you think they are?

A. B. C.

  1 Listen to the conversations. Which picture are the people in? Number the pictures.

 LISTEN AGAIN. Complete the chart. Use the words in the box.

Boston	model	actor
Hollywood	Toronto	student
New York	Vancouver	Miami

	Name	is a/an...	is from...	lives in...
1.	Jane	model		
2.	Joe			
3.	Alice			

2 Listening **PLUS** Listen to more of Jane's conversation. Circle the correct answer.

1. Jane is a model and also a ___.
   a. singer   b. teacher

2. Bob is a ___.
   a. Hollywood producer   b. pilot

3. Bob works for ___.
   a. an airline   b. a very rich man

 *What do they do?*

Student A: Turn to page 85.
Student B: Turn to page 97.

What do you do? • Unit 2

Reading

BEFORE YOU READ Look at the pictures. What is Chuck's job? What is Helen's job?

CD1 Track 18

What Do You Do?
This week—Chuck Hartman and Helen Reed

Chuck Hartman is a **zookeeper** in New York City. He works with lions, tigers, and other big cats. Chuck also works with animals from Australia.

"I work with some very beautiful animals," says Chuck. "Some of them are **dangerous**, but they know me, and they like me—I think!"

Does Chuck like his job? "Do I like my job?" Chuck smiles. "No, I don't like my job. I *love* my job!"

Helen Reed is a **window washer** in London, England. She washes the windows on tall **office buildings** in the city center. She cleans windows eight hours a day, five days a week.

"One of the buildings is 40 **floors** high, and there are more than 5,000 windows," says Helen. "Cleaning the windows is like climbing down a mountain, and the view of London is **fantastic**."

Is she happy at her work? "Happy?" she says. "I'm delighted! It's the best job in the world!"

ONLINE PRACTICE

1 Read the article. Check (✓) *True* or *False*.

	True	False
1. Chuck and Helen work in the same country.	☐	☐
2. Chuck works with lions and tigers.	☐	☐
3. Chuck works in Australia.	☐	☐
4. Helen washes the windows of very tall buildings.	☐	☐
5. Helen climbs mountains at work.	☐	☐
6. Helen thinks her job is boring.	☐	☐

2 GROUP WORK. Do you like the two jobs? Why?

> I like Chuck's job because I like animals!

> I don't like Helen's job because it's dangerous.

Writing
Turn to page 108

14

What do you do? • Unit 2

Conversation PLUS —Jobs survey

1 Which jobs are in the illustration?

```
singer          doctor
chef            teacher
clerk           window washer
zookeeper       architect
office worker   model
soccer player   police officer
```

2 What do you think of the jobs? Complete the chart.

Difficult jobs	Interesting jobs	Tiring jobs	Dangerous jobs
window washer			

3 GROUP WORK. Compare your answers. Who do you agree with?

> I think architects have an interesting job.

> Really? I think it's boring.

> I think they have a difficult job.

4 CLASS ACTIVITY. Share your information with the class.

I think a teacher has a tiring job, but Javier thinks…

Now I can...

- SPEAKING ☐ say what I do and where I live.
- GRAMMAR ☐ use *wh-* questions.
- LISTENING ☐ understand short conversations about people.
- READING ☐ understand short descriptions of jobs.

3 Do you like spicy food?

SPEAKING	GRAMMAR	LISTENING	READING
Likes and dislikes	Simple present	Ordering in restaurants	Eating out

 Warm UP What foods do you like?

Vocabulary

1 Look at the picture. What are the foods? Write the correct letter.

a. lettuce	i. soup
b. onions	j. beans
c. chicken	k. cheese
d. salmon	l. shrimp
e. noodles	m. beef
f. tomato	n. tuna
g. carrots	o. rice
h. potato	p. bread

CD1 Track 19 Listen and check your answers.

2 Complete the chart. Add one more food from the picture to each list.

Meat	Seafood	Vegetables	Others
beef	salmon	lettuce	cheese

Make flashcards to learn new words.

tomatoes — I like tomatoes in my salad.

Vocabulary TIP

3 CLASS ACTIVITY. Find a classmate who likes each food in the chart.

A Do you like <u>chicken</u>?
B Yes.

A What's your name?
B Nino.

Do you like spicy food? • Unit 3

Conversation

1 Complete the conversation. Then listen and check your answers.

a. Let's have dumplings.   b. Chinese   c. pizza

Anthony Are you hungry?
Ana   Hungry? I'm starving!
Anthony Do you like 1 _c_ ?
Ana   No, not really. Do you like 2 _b_ food?
Anthony Yes, I do. I love it!
Ana   3 _a_
Anthony Great idea!
Ana   OK! Let's go!

Now practice the conversation with a partner.

2 PAIR WORK. Practice the conversation again. Use the ideas below. Add your own ideas.

hamburgers	Italian	How about lasagna?
sandwiches	Mexican	Why don't we get tacos?
_____	_____	_____

Do you like spicy food? • Unit 3

Language Practice

The simple present — Grammar Reference page 125

Do you like fish?	Yes, I do.	No, I don't.
Does Chuck like noodles?	Yes, he does.	No, he doesn't.
Do they like pizza?	Yes, they do.	No, they don't.

I **like** shrimp, but I **don't like** salmon.
Dora **likes** chicken, but she **doesn't like** beef.
Dora and Chuck **like** beans, but they **don't like** noodles.

1 Use the chart. Complete the sentences.

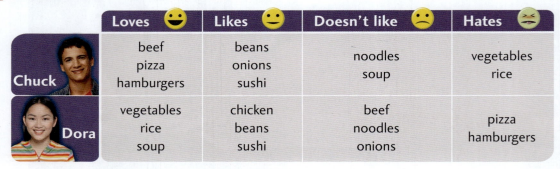

1. Chuck __loves__ hamburgers, but Dora __hates__ them.
2. Dora __Doesn't__ onions, but Chuck __like__ them.
3. Chuck and Dora __Doesn't__ noodles, but they __like__ sushi.
4. A __Does__ Dora __like__ pizza?
   B No, she __not os__ it.
5. A __Do__ Chuck __hate__ vegetables?
   B Yes, he __Do__. But Dora __hates__ them.

2 PAIR WORK. Write three more questions about Chuck and Dora. Then ask and answer the questions.

1. Do Chuck and Dora like beef?   3. _____
2. _____   4. _____

Pronunciation—*Question intonation*

1 Listen. Notice the rising intonation at the end of *yes/no* questions. Then notice the falling intonation at the end of *wh-* questions.

1. Do you like pizza?   3. What kind of food do you like?
2. Do you like Chinese food?   4. What kind of ice cream do you like?

2 Listen again and repeat. Be sure to use rising and falling intonation correctly.

Do you like spicy food? • Unit 3

Listening

BEFORE YOU LISTEN Look at the pictures. What kinds of restaurants are they?

A.

B.

C.

1 Listen to the conversations. Which restaurant are the people in? Number the pictures.

◀◀ LISTEN AGAIN. What do they order? Circle the correct answer.

NEW ASIA

beef and rice	$9.50
noodles	$7.50
chicken soup	$6.25
tuna sushi	$7.00
shrimp sushi	$5.00
rice	$1.50

1.

Cafe ROMA

spaghetti	$10.75
lasagna	$7.50
chicken salad	$6.50
cheese sandwich	$4.00
pizza	$3.00
soup	$3.25

2.

Donna's Diner

hamburger	$7.75
cheeseburger	$8.75
club sandwich	$6.50
tuna sandwich	$5.50
salad	$4.25
onion soup	$4.00
french fries	$3.25

3.

2 Listening PLUS Listen to the people after they order. Complete the chart.

	Does he/she like the food?	What does he/she want?
1.	No, it's salty.	
2.		
3.		

 *Does he like fish?*

Student A: Turn to page 86.
Student B: Turn to page 98.

19

Do you like spicy food? • Unit 3

Reading

BEFORE YOU READ Look at the article. What do you think the article is about?

CD1 Track 25

Eating out in ...

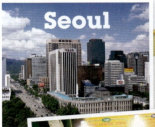
Seoul

kimchi

Kimchi is Korea's best-known food. It's made from cabbage, chili peppers, and vegetables. Korean restaurants serve it at almost every meal. It's difficult to **describe**—there are so many different types!

Seoul has great restaurants, but there is also cheap and interesting food on the streets. You can get **delicious** *kimbap* (rice and seaweed rolls) and *dukbokki* (rice cakes in a hot pepper sauce) from food carts called *pojangmacha*. It's a good value and you get a lot! We also **recommend** the chicken kebabs and the dumplings.

pojangmacha

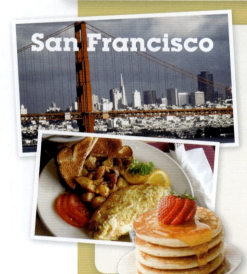
San Francisco

San Francisco offers the best of world cuisine, including some **fascinating** mixtures of styles—Japanese-Italian, Korean-American, and so on. But what do San Francisco people like best? Sunday brunch!

The best and often the biggest **meal** of the week is brunch. At many restaurants, there is a long table full of wonderful food: eggs, pancakes, sandwiches, salmon, and home fries (fried potatoes you eat with breakfast). You can have breakfast food for lunch—or lunch food for breakfast! That's why it's called *brunch* (breakfast + lunch).

Did you know? Ninety-five percent of San Francisco's restaurants have doggy bags (**take-out** containers for the food you don't finish), because "today's brunch is tomorrow's lunch."

Sunday brunch

ONLINE PRACTICE

1 Read the article. Match the words and definitions.

1. *kimchi* ___
2. *pojangmacha* ___
3. *brunch* ___
4. *doggy bag* ___

a. a box for food you don't finish
b. a meal with breakfast and lunch dishes
c. street food carts
d. a well-known Korean food

 2 GROUP WORK. What food in the article do you want to try? Tell your group.

> I want to try home fries because I like potatoes. How about you?

> I want to try kimchi. I like spicy food!

Writing
Turn to page 109

Do you like spicy food? • Unit 3

Conversation PLUS —Your favorite food

1 What foods do you like? Look at the questions in the survey. Then write your answers.

	You	Student 1	Student 2
1. What is your favorite food?			
2. What is your favorite drink?			
3. What foreign food do you like? (American, Italian …)			
4. What new food do you want to try?			
5. What food do you hate?			
6. What food can you cook?			
7. Do you like spicy food?			

2 GROUP WORK. Ask and answer the questions. Complete the survey.

What is your favorite food?

Pizza. What is your favorite food?

Sushi. What is your favorite drink?

3 GROUP WORK. Look at the restaurants. Which one is the best for your group? Why? Share your ideas with the class.

A We like <u>beef</u>, so let's go to the <u>Mexican restaurant</u>.
B Yes, but I don't like <u>cheese</u>. How about the <u>Chinese restaurant</u>?
C That sounds good. Let's go!

Diner   Chinese restaurant

Mexican restaurant

Now I can...

- **SPEAKING** ☐ talk about my likes and dislikes.
- **GRAMMAR** ☐ use the simple present.
- **LISTENING** ☐ understand short conversations about ordering.
- **READING** ☐ understand short texts about eating out.

Review Units 1-3

1 Read the conversation. Circle the correct answer.

Sophia	Hi, I'm Sophia. Nice to meet you.
Carlos	Hi, I'm Carlos. Nice to meet you, Sophia. (Are you)/ You are a friend of Alex?
Sophia	Yes, we're teachers at the same school.
Carlos	Oh, that's great!
Sophia	Thanks. Where are / Where you from, Carlos?
Carlos	I'm from Mexico. [SAY MORE]
Sophia	Really? My brother works in Mexico.
Carlos	What does he do?
Sophia	He's a doctor. What about you? What do / does you do?
Carlos	I'm an architect.
Sophia	Oh! My sister is an architect.
Carlos	Really? Where does she live?
Sophia	She lives / live in Canada. [SAY MORE]
Carlos	Are you Canadian?
Sophia	No, my family is from the US.
Carlos	I see. Do / Are you live here in the city?
Sophia	Only in the summer. I work in Japan in the winter. [SAY MORE]
Carlos	Wow, that's interesting.

Listen and check your answers. Then practice the conversation with a partner.

2 PAIR WORK. Put a box around the jobs and countries. Practice the conversation again. Use your own ideas for the jobs and countries.

3 Practice the conversation again. This time add information and [SAY MORE].

Sophia	Where are / Where you from, Carlos?
Carlos	I'm from Mexico. [I live in Guadalajara.]

Review • Units 1–3

4 Look at the article. Who is it about?

CITY SPOTLIGHT

Meet New York's best new chef!

LUIS SILVA IS A CHEF. HE LIVES IN MANHATTAN AND WORKS AT CRUZ'S GRILL ON 6TH AVENUE.

Where are you from?
I'm from São Paulo, Brazil, but I live in New York now.

Why did you become a chef?
I love food, and my mother is a wonderful cook!

Is your mother a chef, too?
No, she isn't. She's a teacher, but sometimes I wish she could work in my restaurant!

What kind of food do you like?
I like all kinds of food—Chinese, Italian, Mexican. But Japanese food is probably my favorite.

What's your favorite Japanese restaurant in the city?
Oh, that's a hard question. Hmm… I think Mika. They have the best noodles, and their sushi is very good, too. But my wife's favorite is Tokyo House.

What about other kinds of restaurants?
For Chinese food, I like House of Ping on Grant Street. I always have the chicken soup there. And I really like Primo's on 30th Street for Italian. On Mondays, they have a spaghetti special, and it's delicious. But don't ask me about places for pizza. I don't like it!

And what about Mexican restaurants? What's your favorite?
Oh, definitely Julio's on 2nd Street. My friend Manuel is the chef there. He's from Mexico City, so it's real Mexican food. Actually, his mother is a chef, too. Her restaurant is on 45th Street, but she makes Spanish food. Manuel and I like to eat there when we're not working.

5 Read the article. Check (✓) *True* or *False*.

	True	False
1. Luis is from Brazil.	☐	☐
2. His mother is a chef.	☐	☐
3. His favorite Japanese restaurant is Tokyo House.	☐	☐
4. Luis's favorite Chinese restaurant is Grant's.	☐	☐
5. He likes the spaghetti at Primo's.	☐	☐
6. Luis likes the pizza at Primo's.	☐	☐
7. Luis's friend Julio is a chef at a Mexican restaurant.	☐	☐
8. His friend has a Spanish restaurant on 45th Street.	☐	☐

 6 GROUP WORK. What are your favorite restaurants? What foods do you like at these restaurants? Tell your group.

| SPEAKING | GRAMMAR | LISTENING | READING |
| Habits and routines | Frequency adverbs | Leisure activities | City attractions |

How often do you do yoga?

 What are your favorite sports?

lifting

Vocabulary

1 Look at the picture. What are the sports activities? Write the correct letter.

a. swimming   e. basketball
b. soccer   f. martial arts
c. bicycling   g. jogging
d. weightlifting h. yoga

1. e
2. h
3. a
4. d
5. f
6. b
7. c
8. g

CD1 Track 28 Listen and check your answers.

2 Complete the chart with the activities in the picture.

Go...	Do...	Play...
swimming	martial arts	soccer

3 PAIR WORK. Do you do the activities? Tell your partner.

A Do you <u>go swimming</u>?
B Yes, I do. Do you <u>do yoga</u>?
C No, I don't. Do you ... ?

24

How often do you do yoga? • Unit 4

Conversation

1 Complete the conversation. Then listen and check your answers.

> a. yoga   b. tennis   c. swimming   d. I love it!

Brad Clare, you're in great shape. What do you do to keep fit?
Clare I go 1 _____, or I do 2 _____.
Brad How often do you do that?
Clare Every morning. 3 _____
Brad Wow! How often do you go to the gym?
Clare Ugh! I never go to the gym. I hate it. It's too crowded.
Brad I see.
Clare And what about you? What do you do to keep fit?
Brad I usually go to the gym after work, and I play 4 _____ about twice a week.

Now practice the conversation with a partner.

2 PAIR WORK. Practice the conversation again. Use the ideas below. Add your own ideas.

bicycling	martial arts	It's great.	basketball
jogging	weightlifting	It's a lot of fun.	soccer
___	___	___	___

TAKING TURNS
Ask questions to let your partner talk.

How often do you go to the gym?

I never go. How about you?

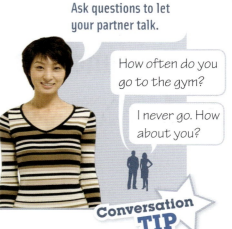

Conversation TIP

25

How often do you do yoga? • Unit 4

Language Practice

Frequency adverbs and time expressions Grammar Reference page 126

Do you ever exercise after class?
Yes, I **always** go jogging after school.
Yes, I **usually** play tennis with my friend.
Yes, I **sometimes** go swimming, but
I **never** do yoga.

How often do you exercise?
I go jogging **every day**.
I play tennis **four times a week**.
I go swimming **once a week**.

	M	Tu	W	Th	F	Sa	Su
jogging	✓	✓	✓	✓	✓	✓	✓
tennis		✓		✓		✓	✓
swimming			✓				
yoga							

1 Look at the information about Anna. Then complete the sentences.

	M	Tu	W	Th	F	Sa	Su
jogging	✓			✓			
tennis							
swimming	✓	✓	✓	✓	✓	✓	✓
yoga		✓	✓		✓		✓

1. Anna __usually__ does yoga.
2. She _____ plays tennis.
3. She goes jogging _____.
4. She goes swimming _____.
5. She _____ goes jogging.
6. She does yoga _____.

2 PAIR WORK. Complete the conversations. Use your own ideas.

1. A Do you ever _____?
   B Yes, I do.
   A Really? How often _____?
   B _____.

2. A Do you ever _____?
   B No, I don't. But I like _____.
   A Really? How often _____?
   B _____.

Pronunciation–*Final s sounds*

1 Listen. Notice how the final s sounds like /s/ or /z/. Does each word end in a /s/ or /z/? Write s or z.

1. _s_ tenni**s**
2. ___ alway**s**
3. ___ cla**ss**
4. ___ sometime**s**
5. ___ swim**s**
6. ___ martial art**s**

2 Listen again and repeat. Be sure to say the final s correctly.

26

Listening

BEFORE YOU LISTEN Look at the people. What do you think they do for fun?

A.

B.

C.

1 Listen to the interviews. Which person is it? Number the pictures.

◀◀ **LISTEN AGAIN.** Complete the chart.

	Name	Age	Activity	Frequency
1.	Greg		goes swimming	
2.	Alice	27		
3.	Tom			every Wednesday

2 Listening PLUS Listen to more of the interviews. Check (✓) *True* or *False*.

		True	False
1.	Greg never swims at the beach in the winter.	☐	☐
2.	Greg goes jogging every day in the winter.	☐	☐
3.	Alice goes to the gym when it's not crowded.	☐	☐
4.	Tom likes the gym because there are young people.	☐	☐

Smart TALK *How often?*

Student A: Turn to page 87.
Student B: Turn to page 99.

How often do you do yoga? • Unit 4

Reading

BEFORE YOU READ Look at the title and picture. What do you think the article is about?

CD1
Track 34

YOU WANT TO PLAY IN THE NBA?

Read on …

Basketball is a very popular sport all over the world. Young **players** from all countries dream of becoming **professional** players, and they want to play in the best **league** in the world, the NBA (National Basketball Association).

What's it like playing at the top level of this amazing sport?

Professional basketball is a hard, non-stop sport, and the players are very tall and fast. They need a lot of energy, and they need to be very fit. They never stop **training**—in the gym, on the running track, and on the court. When the **season** starts in October, training gets *really* serious.

Chinese superstar Yao Ming trains seven days a week during the season, and he often trains alone. In the morning, he usually spends an hour in the gym before he meets his **teammates**. He warms up and shoots baskets. He always shoots at least 200 baskets, and he sometimes shoots more than a thousand! He never stops practicing.

Do you want to be a professional basketball player? Do you want to train like an NBA superstar?

Yao Ming

ONLINE PRACTICE

1 Read the article. Complete the questions. Then match them with the answers.

1. When does the NBA _____ start? ____
2. Do players stop _____? ____
3. How _____ does Yao Ming train? ____
4. How many baskets does Yao Ming _____ shoot? ____

a. No, never.
b. Seven days a week.
c. 200 baskets.
d. In October.

2 Read the article again. Check (✓) *True* or *False*.

	True	False
1. NBA players start training in October.	☐	☐
2. NBA players train in many places.	☐	☐
3. Superstar players always train alone.	☐	☐
4. Yao Ming trains every day during the season.	☐	☐

3 GROUP WORK. Do you watch professional sports on TV? Which ones?

I sometimes watch baseball on TV.

I never watch baseball, but I often watch soccer.

Writing
Turn to page 109

28

How often do you do yoga? • Unit 4

Conversation PLUS —Do you ever play soccer?

1 PAIR WORK. How often do you play sports or exercise? Tell your partner.

I usually play tennis. I sometimes go swimming, but I never do weightlifting.

2 CLASS ACTIVITY. Find classmates who do the activities in the chart. Write their names and try to get extra information!

A Do you <u>play soccer</u>?
B Yes, I do.
A How often do you <u>play soccer</u>?
B I <u>play every week</u>. <u>I love it</u>!

NAME		EXTRA INFORMATION
1. _____	plays soccer every week.	_____
2. _____	sometimes goes bicycling.	_____
3. _____	goes skiing every winter.	_____
4. _____	never does weightlifting.	_____
5. _____	plays tennis every summer.	_____
6. _____	never does yoga.	_____
7. _____	sometimes goes swimming.	_____
8. _____	goes jogging every day.	_____
9. _____	usually does martial arts.	_____
10. _____	never exercises.	_____

3 CLASS ACTIVITY. Share your information with the class.

Carlos plays soccer every week.

Aya plays soccer, too.

Tim never plays soccer. He never exercises.

Now I can...

SPEAKING ☐ talk about habits and routines.
GRAMMAR ☐ use frequency adverbs and time expressions.
LISTENING ☐ understand descriptions of leisure activities.
READING ☐ understand descriptions of city attractions.

5 What are you watching?

SPEAKING Daily activities
GRAMMAR Present continuous
LISTENING Describing activities
READING Cell phone rules

 What is one thing you do every day?

Vocabulary

a. do homework
b. send a text message
c. play a computer game
d. check e-mail
e. read a magazine
f. listen to music
g. talk on the phone
h. watch TV
i. take a nap

1 Look at the people. What are they doing? Write the correct letter.

CD1 Track 35 — Listen and check your answers.

2 Complete the phrases.

1. <u>t</u>ak<u>e</u> a <u>n</u>a p
2. ___ d a _aga____
3. l____n to ____c
4. _o _o___o__

3 PAIR WORK. How often do you do the things in Activity 1? Tell your partner.

A I <u>check my e-mail</u> every day. How often do you <u>check your e-mail</u>?
B I <u>check my e-mail</u> every day, too.

Make lists of words that follow the same verb

do homework
do yoga
do martial arts

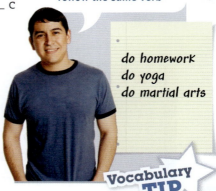

Vocabulary TIP

30

What are you watching? • Unit 5

Conversation

ONLINE PRACTICE

 1 Complete the conversation. Then listen and check your answers.

> a. China   b. English   c. *Harry Potter*

Kelly   Hello?
Emily   Hey, Kelly! It's Emily. What are you doing?
Kelly   I'm studying. What are you doing?
Emily   I'm studying, too. What are you studying?
Kelly   1 ____b____ . How about you?
Emily   I'm reading a book about 2 ____a____ .
Kelly   That's nice. Actually, I'm not studying.
Emily   Yeah, me neither. I'm watching a movie.
Kelly   Me, too! What are you watching?
Emily   I'm watching 3 ____c____ .
Kelly   No way! Me too!

Now practice the conversation with a partner.

 2 PAIR WORK. Practice the conversation again. Use the ideas below. Add your own ideas.

history	Africa	*Lord of the Rings*
math	Canada	*Transformers*
_____	_____	_____

31

What are you watching? • Unit 5

Language Practice

The present continuous — Grammar Reference page 127

Are you **studying**?	Yes, I **am**.	No, **I'm not**.
Is she **studying**?	Yes, **she is**.	No, she **isn't**.
Are they **studying**?	Yes, they **are**.	No, they **aren't**.

What **are** you **doing**?	**I'm watching** a movie.	
What **is** she **doing**?	**She's watching** a movie.	She **isn't studying**.
What **are** they **doing**?	**They're watching** TV.	They **aren't doing** homework.

1 Complete the conversations.

1. A What's your sister doing?
   B She __'s having__ lunch.

2. A What's your friend doing?
   B He __is__ (checking) his e-mail.

3. A What are you doing?
   B I __am__ (reading), a book about Korea.

4. A What are they doing?
   B They __are__ (talking) on the phone.

2 Complete the sentences. Use the verbs in the box.

| talk | play | read | take |

1. What book are you __reading__?
2. She's with her friends. I think she __is playing__ soccer.
3. He's busy now. He __is taking__ on the phone.
4. She's at home. She __is taking__ a nap.

3 PAIR WORK. What do you think your friends and family are doing now? Tell your partner.

> What's your best friend doing now?

> I'm not sure. Maybe she's watching TV.

Pronunciation—*Reduction of* what is *and* what are

1 Listen. Notice the reduced sounds of *what is* and *what are*.

Unreduced	Reduced
1. What's your teacher doing?	Whatsyar teacher doing?
2. What's your mom eating?	Whatsyar mom eating?
3. What are you doing?	Whadaya doing?
4. What are you reading?	Whadaya reading?

2 Listen again and repeat. Be sure to say the reduced sounds.

Listening

BEFORE YOU LISTEN Look at the people. What are they doing?

A.

B.

C.

D.

E.

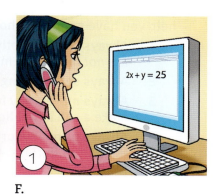
F.

1 Listen to the phone calls. Which two people are talking? Number the pictures.

◀◀ LISTEN AGAIN. Answer the questions.

1. What is Joe watching on TV?
2. Are both Susie and Maria reading interesting things?
3. What does Richard think about his homework?
4. What does Richard want to do?

2 Listening PLUS Listen to more of Diane and Joe's call. Circle the correct answer.

1. Diane is ____.
   a. Joe's mother
   b. Joe's tutor

2. Joe is good at math, ____.
   a. and he works hard
   b. but he doesn't work hard

3. Joe tells Diane ____.
   a. she looks 18
   b. he's looking at page 18

Smart TALK — *What is he doing?*

Student A: Turn to page 88.
Student B: Turn to page 100.

What are you watching? • Unit 5

Reading

BEFORE YOU READ Look at the pictures. What are the people doing wrong?

Do you have good cell phone manners?

Cell phones are wonderful! You can talk to your friends while you're watching TV or when you're sitting in a coffee shop. People can **contact** you with important news all the time.

But be careful! Sometimes cell phones cause problems for the people around you. Here are eight suggestions to help you have good cell phone manners.

1. **Always** speak quietly on the phone. Other people are *not* interested in your conversations.
2. **Always** set your **ring tone** at a low level.
3. **Always** move away from other people when you make a call **in public**.
4. **Always** turn off your phone at the movies, in a theater, or in class. If you can't turn it off, switch to **vibrate**.
5. **Never** send a text message in class.
6. **Never** talk on the phone when you are buying something in a store or checking in at an airport. It isn't **polite**.
7. **Never** use your phone on a plane or in a hospital. It can cause problems with their **technology**.
8. **Never** choose a really bad pop song as your ring tone!

ONLINE PRACTICE

1 Read the article. Are these good ideas or bad ideas? Mark them G (good idea) or B (bad idea).

1. moving away from people when you're making a call _G_
2. turning off your phone in a theater ___
3. talking on the phone when you're buying something ___
4. using your cell phone on an airplane ___
5. using a bad pop song as a ring tone ___

2 GROUP WORK. What do you think are bad cell phone manners? Tell your group.

> It's bad manners when people talk loudly on their phones in a store.

> I don't like it when people send text messages and I'm talking to them!

Writing Turn to page 110

What are you watching? • Unit 5

Conversation PLUS —Cell phone habits

1 How do you use your cell phone? Take the survey. Be honest!

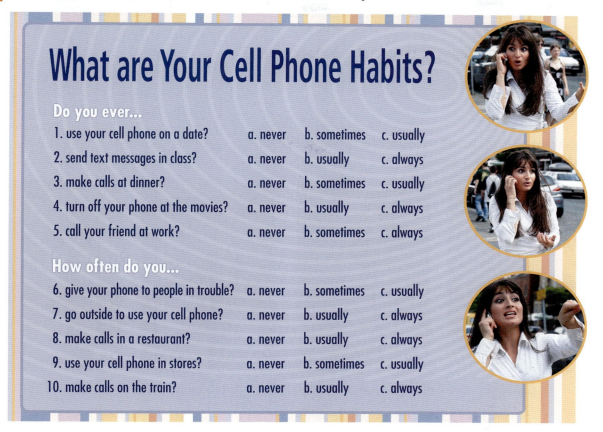

2 GROUP WORK. Compare your answers. Who has the best cell phone habits? Give your opinions about them.

> Do you ever use your cell phone on a date?

> I never use my cell phone on a date! I think it's rude.

> I do sometimes, but only if I'm bored!

3 CLASS ACTIVITY. Discuss the questions.
1. Which cell phone habits are always a bad idea?
2. Which cell phone habits are sometimes a bad idea?
3. Which cell phone habits are OK all the time?

Now I can...
- SPEAKING ☐ talk about what people are doing.
- GRAMMAR ☐ use the present continuous.
- LISTENING ☐ understand descriptions of daily activities.
- READING ☐ understand rules for polite cell phone use.

| SPEAKING | GRAMMAR | LISTENING | READING |
| Past events | Past tense of *be* | Problems | Past and present |

Where were you yesterday?

 Do the things in the pictures happen to you?

Vocabulary

a. broken	e. The weather
b. The traffic	f. lost
c. late	g. The lines
d. crowded	h. sick

1 Look at the pictures. Complete the sentences. Write the correct letter.

1. He's __late__. 2. _____ is terrible. 3. He's _____. 4. His cell phone is _____.

5. _____ are long. 6. The bus is _____. 7. _____ is awful. 8. He's _____.

CD1 Track 42 — Listen and check your answers.

 2 PAIR WORK. What is happening to the man? Use the pictures to tell a story.

He's late for English class because the weather is terrible, and he's lost. He wants to call his friend to ask for directions, but ...

36

Where were you yesterday? • Unit 6

Conversation

 1 Complete the conversation. Then listen and check your answers.

> a. bus   b. watch   c. sick

Teacher Good morning, Marco.
Marco Good morning. Sorry I'm late. My [1 b] was broken.
Teacher Was it broken yesterday, too?
Marco Yesterday?
Teacher Remember, you were also late yesterday!
Marco Oh, no. I was late yesterday because the [2 a] was crowded.
Teacher Interesting. And you weren't here last week. How come?
Marco I was [3 c].
Teacher I see. And do you have your homework?
Marco Homework?

Now practice the conversation with a partner.

 2 PAIR WORK. Practice the conversation again. Use the ideas below. Add your own ideas.

bicycle	train	at work
alarm clock	station	on vacation
_____	_____	_____

GETTING CLARIFICATION
Get more explanation by repeating what your partner said

Where were you yesterday? • Unit 6

Language Practice

The past tense of *be*		Grammar Reference page 128
Were you at home?	Yes, I **was**.	No, I **wasn't**.
Was she in class?	Yes, she **was**.	No, she **wasn't**.
Were they on vacation?	Yes, they **were**.	No, they **weren't**.
Where **were** you yesterday?	I **was** at home.	I **wasn't** in class.
Where **was** he yesterday?	He **was** at home.	He **wasn't** in class.
Where **were** they yesterday?	They **were** at home.	They **weren't** in class.

CD1 Track 44

ONLINE PRACTICE

1 Complete the conversations.

1. A ___Was___ Michelle in class yesterday?
   B No, she ___wasn't___. She ___was___ sick.
2. A Where ___was___ your brother yesterday?
   B He ___was___ at home.
3. A Why ___wasn't___ you at school yesterday?
   B Because we ___were___ sick.

2 Complete the sentences with information about you.

1. I ___wasn't___ late for class today.
2. I ___wasn't___ at home this time yesterday.
3. I ___wasn't___ at a soccer game last Saturday.
4. I ___wasn't___ on vacation last July.

3 PAIR WORK. Ask and answer questions about the past.

1. Were you in class yesterday? _____
2. Were you at home at 8 p.m. last night? _____
3. Were you on vacation last week? _____
4. Were you at this school last year? _____

Pronunciation—*Reduction of* t *in* wasn't *and* weren't

CD1 Track 45

1 Listen. Notice how the final t can be reduced when *wasn't* or *weren't* are followed by a vowel sound.

Unreduced	Reduced
1. He wasn't at home.	He *wazn* at home.
2. They weren't at a concert.	They *wern* at a concert.
3. I wasn't in class yesterday.	I *wazn* in class yesterday.
4. You weren't on vacation.	You *wern* on vacation.

2 Listen again and repeat. Be sure to say the reduced sounds.

38

Where were you yesterday? • Unit 6

Listening

BEFORE YOU LISTEN   Look at the people. Where are they?

A.

B.

C.

  1 Listen to the conversations. Number the pictures.

⏪ LISTEN AGAIN. Why were the people late? Circle the correct answer.

1. a. He was sick.
   b. The traffic was terrible.
   c. The plane was late.

2. a. Her bus was late.
   b. She was busy.
   c. She was in the kitchen.

3. a. He was on the phone.
   b. He was at the beach.
   c. He was at the mountains.

2 Listening PLUS Listen to more of the man at the airport. Circle the correct answer.

1. Why does the check-in clerk say, "Calm down"?
   a. Because the man is angry.
   b. Because the man is panicking.

2. Where was the man before he was at the airport?
   a. He was at home.
   b. He was in a hotel.

3. Where is the man's ticket?
   a. It's on the table in his hotel room.
   b. It's on the floor by the check-in desk.

 *Where were they?*

Student A: Turn to page 89.
Student B: Turn to page 101.

39

Where were you yesterday? • Unit 6

Reading

BEFORE YOU READ Look at the picture. What do you think the article is about?

CD1 Track 48

OVERNIGHT SUCCESS!

Three months ago, they were an unknown band, playing in small clubs. This week, their song "Sitting in the Kitchen" is at the top of the charts. Meet The Smarts!

Hello, I'm Carrie Stewart, and I'm the bass player with the band. Last year, I was in an all-girl band called Daisy Park. I prefer being in The Smarts!

Hi, my name's Carl Robinson. I'm one of the singers with The Smarts. Last year, I was a taxi driver, and now I'm in the best band in the world!

Hello, my name is Ellie May Robinson. I'm Carl's sister, and I'm also a vocalist with The Smarts. I was a hotel receptionist before I joined the band. I like singing better!

I'm Joe Fish, and I'm the drummer with the band. Before I joined The Smarts, I was a drummer with another band. Drumming is my life!

Hi, I'm Billy Tao, and I'm the guitarist with the band. Joe, the drummer, is my best friend. Before we were in The Smarts, we were in another band called The Easytones.

Carrie   Carl   Ellie May   Joe   Billy

ONLINE PRACTICE

1 Read the article. Match the people to what they do in the band.

1. Carl ___
2. Ellie May ___
3. Joe ___
4. Billy ___
5. Carrie ___

a. plays drums
b. sings
c. plays guitar
d. plays bass
e. sings

2 Read the article again. Check (✓) *True* or *False*.

Before they were in The Smarts…	True	False
1. Two band members were together in another band.	☐	☐
2. Carl's sister was in a band called Daisy Park.	☐	☐
3. Carl was a taxi driver.	☐	☐
4. Ellie May was a receptionist.	☐	☐

3 GROUP WORK. Which bands do you like? What do you know about them?

> I'm a Sting fan. Sting was in a band called The Police.

> I love the Beatles. Their first album was *Please Please Me*.

Writing Turn to page 110

40

Where were you yesterday? • Unit 6

Conversation PLUS —Where were you?

1 Look at the questions in the survey. Add two more questions. Then write your answers.

	You	Student 1	Student 2
Where were you …			
1. at this time yesterday?			
2. at this time last week?			
3. last Saturday night?			
4. on your last birthday?			
5. on December 31 last year?			
6. (your choice) _____			
Who were you with …			
1. last week?			
2. last Saturday night?			
3. on your last birthday?			
4. on January 1 this year?			
5. on vacation last year?			
6. (your choice) _____			

2 GROUP WORK. Ask and answer the questions. Complete the survey.

> Where were you at this time yesterday?

> I was at the park near school.

3 CLASS ACTIVITY. Share your information with the class.

Jun was in Chicago on December 31 last year.

Now I can...

- **SPEAKING** ☐ talk about past events.
- **GRAMMAR** ☐ use the simple past of *be*.
- **LISTENING** ☐ understand short conversations about problems.
- **READING** ☐ understand an article about past and present.

Review Units 4-6

1 Read the conversation. Circle the correct answer.

Ava	Ethan, this is Ava. Where are you?
Ethan	I'm at home. [SAY MORE]
Ava	What *you are / are you* doing? 　　　　　1
Ethan	I'm checking my e-mail, and I'm listening to some music.
Ava	Why *weren't / wasn't* you in class this morning?　　　2
Ethan	Because the weather was terrible, and the bus was crowded.
Ava	Ethan, you *always have / have always* the same excuse. You're just lazy!　　3
Ethan	No, I'm not! And actually, now I'm sick. [SAY MORE]
Ava	Really?
Ethan	Yes! Anyway, where are you? Are you in class?
Ava	No, I *was / were* in class, but now I'm at Susie's party.　4
Ethan	Susie *is having / has* a party? 　　　　　　5
Ava	Yes. [SAY MORE]
Ethan	OK! I'm on my way.
Ava	But you're sick.
Ethan	No, it's OK. I'm feeling better!

 Listen and check your answers. Then practice the conversation with a partner.

2 PAIR WORK. Put a box around the excuses. Practice the conversation again. Use your own ideas for the excuses.

3 Practice the conversation again. This time add information and [SAY MORE].

Ava	Ethan, this is Ava. Where are you?
Ethan	I'm at home. [In my room]

42

4 Read the article quickly. How many people does Sally Garcia talk to?

Early Birds
By Sally Garcia

What do you do before sunrise? Do you go jogging? Do you do yoga? Or, like most people, are you in bed until the sun comes up?

It's 5 a.m. It's dark, and I'm sitting in a coffee shop. The place is crowded!

I'm here because I'm writing an article for this magazine, but what are all these other people doing here—at this time in the morning?

Robin is 24, and he's studying to be a lawyer. "What am I doing? I'm checking my e-mail, and I'm doing homework," he says. "I have classes from 8 a.m. to 5 p.m. every day. After that, I go to my sports clubs— martial arts on Mondays, basketball on Tuesdays, yoga on Wednesdays. I never have free time! So I always study here in the mornings."

Helen is a nurse. "I'm chatting online with a friend in Seattle," she says. "I work nights at the hospital, and this is my break. Excuse me, my friend is saying something important…" She's talking to someone in Seattle? What time is it there?

Andy is a taxi driver. "I'm playing computer games," he tells me.

"Why aren't you driving your taxi?" I ask.

"I usually start work at 8 a.m.," he replies.

"So why aren't you sleeping?"

"I drive downtown very early every morning because the traffic is awful later. I leave the car in the parking lot, and I come here. I usually have a coffee and then start work. This is a good place to wait."

There are about 20 people in the coffee shop. They all have similar stories. Now I'm thinking, maybe this is the best place to be at 5 a.m.!

5 Read the article again. Answer the questions.
1. Why is Sally at the coffee shop?
2. Why is Robin at the coffee shop?
3. Who is Helen chatting with?
4. Why does Andy drive downtown very early?

6 GROUP WORK. What do you usually do in the mornings? Tell your group.

| SPEAKING | GRAMMAR | LISTENING | READING |
| Talking about clothes | Comparative adjectives | Clothes shopping | Comparing opinions |

Which one is cheaper?

 What are you wearing right now?

Vocabulary

1 Look at the people. What are they wearing? Write the correct letter.

a. a dress
b. a white shirt
c. baggy pants
d. a nice jacket
e. a colorful sweater
f. high heels
g. a scarf
h. a tie
i. jeans
j. a dark suit
k. a T-shirt
l. sneakers

 Listen and check your answers.

2 PAIR WORK. Ask and answer questions about clothing.

A Do you ever wear <u>a suit</u>?
B No. I never wear <u>a suit</u>. I usually wear <u>jeans</u>.
A Do you like <u>high heels</u>?
B Yes, I do.
A How often do you wear <u>them</u>?
B I wear <u>them</u> <u>every day</u>.

Draw pictures to learn new words.

44

Which one is cheaper? • Unit 7

Conversation

 1 Complete the conversation. Then listen and check your answers.

> a. cooler   b. $150   c. shirt   d. shoes

Kelly	What are you looking for?
Emily	I need a pair of 1 __d__ , but first I need a new 2 __c__ .
Kelly	OK. What about these two? Which one do you prefer?
Emily	Which one is more expensive?
Kelly	The black one.
Emily	How much is it?
Kelly	Wow! It's 3 __b__ .
Emily	Hmm. What about the red one?
Kelly	It's $39.00.
Emily	I think the black one is 4 __a__ than the red one.
Kelly	Yeah. But the red one is cheaper.
Emily	I'm not surprised!

longer

Now practice the conversation with a partner.

 2 PAIR WORK. Practice the conversation again. Use the ideas below. Add your own ideas.

jeans	jacket	$300	better
gloves	scarf	$99	more stylish
___	___	___	___

45

Which one is cheaper? • Unit 7

Language Practice

Comparative adjectives — CD2 Track 4 — Grammar Reference page 129

The red dress is **cheaper than** the black one.
The black dress is**n't as cheap** as the red one.

The black dress is **more expensive than** the red one.
The red dress is**n't as expensive as** the red one.
Which one is **cheaper**?   The red one.

good → **better**
bad → **worse**

ONLINE PRACTICE

1 Complete the sentences. Use the adjective in parentheses.

1. Regular jeans are ____cheaper than____ designer jeans. (cheap)
2. Old shoes are _____ new ones. (comfortable)
3. Her dress is _____ your black one. (colorful)
4. This scarf is _____ that dirty one. (nice)

2 Now rewrite the sentences. Use *not as … as …*

1. Designer jeans _aren't as cheap as_ regular jeans.
2. These new shoes _____ my old ones.
3. Your black dress _____ hers.
4. That dirty scarf _____ this one.

3 PAIR WORK. Do you agree or disagree with the sentences? If you disagree, give your opinion.

1. Designer clothes are more comfortable than regular clothes.
2. Sneakers aren't as comfortable as high heels.
3. A suit is cooler than jeans and a T-shirt.

> Designer clothes are more comfortable than regular clothes.

> I disagree. I think regular clothes are more comfortable.

Pronunciation—*Word stress in comparisons*

1 Listen. Notice the stress on words that are compared. — CD2 Track 5

1. The <u>black</u> bag is cooler than the <u>red</u> one.
2. My <u>new</u> phone is cheaper than my <u>old</u> one.
3. <u>Your</u> shoes are newer than <u>mine</u>.
4. My <u>jeans</u> are more comfortable than my <u>skirt</u>.

2 Listen again and repeat. Be sure to stress the words correctly.

46

Listening

BEFORE YOU LISTEN Look at the pictures. How are the clothes different?

A.

B.

C.

D.

 1 Listen to people shopping. What are they looking for? Number the pictures.

⏪ LISTEN AGAIN. Which item do they decide to buy? Circle the correct answer.

1. a. the designer jeans
   b. the regular jeans

2. a. the expensive shoes
   b. the cheaper shoes

3. a. the Italian jacket
   b. the blue jacket

4. a. the red sweater
   b. the expensive sweater

 2 Listening PLUS Listen to more of the first two customers. Check (✓) True or False.

	True	False
1. At first, the first customer wants the cheaper jeans.	☐	☐
2. In the end, the first customer buys the cheaper jeans.	☐	☐
3. At first, the second customer wants the expensive shoes.	☐	☐
4. In the end, the second customer buys the cheaper shoes.	☐	☐

 *Which one do you like?*

Student A: Turn to page 90.
Student B: Turn to page 102.

Which one is cheaper? • Unit 7

Reading

BEFORE YOU READ How many designer labels do you know? Which countries do they come from?

CD2 Track 8

Designer jeans—are they worth it?

Kevin Kern is 28 years old, and he's a hairdresser. His usual **outfit** is jeans and a T-shirt when he's working and in his free time. But believe it or not, Kevin **spends** $5,000 a year on clothes. He likes designer jeans that cost $400. His favorite T-shirt cost $200. He has five $200 T-shirts!

"Most of my T-shirts are much less expensive than that," he says. "I saw a John Galliano T-shirt that was really cool. It had **huge** dollar signs on it. It cost $535. Now that's too expensive for me!"

A pair of regular jeans costs $50. So, why do people like Kevin buy designer jeans for $400?

Fashion **expert** Mitsui Kodah says, "Some people buy designer jeans and T-shirts because they think they look better. Other people think designer jeans are better **quality**. And some people buy them because they have a famous designer's name on them."

"Designer jeans are definitely a lot more comfortable," says Kevin. "But for me, it isn't about the name. I like the way they look, I like the way they feel—and I like the name, too, I guess."

Fashion writer Max Walter says, "Young people want to be cool, and designer **brands** are cool. Plus designer jeans look better than regular jeans. That's for sure!"

ONLINE PRACTICE

1 Read the article. What does the money refer to?

| $50 | $200 | $400 | $535 | $5,000 |

2 Read the article again. Circle the correct answer.

1. Kevin wears T-shirts and jeans ___.
   a. when he's working   b. all the time

2. Kevin likes designer jeans because ___.
   a. they are comfortable   b. they are expensive

3. According to a fashion expert, people buy designer jeans ___.
   a. only because of the name   b. for several reasons

4. Max Walter thinks that designer jeans ___ than regular jeans.
   a. look better   b. are more comfortable

 3 GROUP WORK. Do you like designer clothes? Why or why not?

> I like designer clothes because they look better.

> Me, too, but they're too expensive!

Writing
Turn to page 111

48

Which one is cheaper? • Unit 7

Conversation PLUS —Fashion survey

1 Look at the questions in the survey. Then write your answers.

	You	Your partner	Extra information
1. What do you wear to school?			
2. What do you wear when you go out?			
3. What do you wear on the weekend?			
4. How often do you wear jeans?			
5. Where do you buy your clothes?			
6. Which designer labels do you like?			

2 PAIR WORK. Ask and answer the questions. Complete the survey. Try to give extra information!

What do you wear to school?

I usually wear jeans and a T-shirt. How about you?

I always wear a school uniform. I hate it!

3 CLASS ACTIVITY. Share your information with the class. Then complete the sentences.

Almost all of us wear jeans on the weekend.

1. All of us _____.
2. Almost all of us _____.
3. Some of us _____.
4. A few of us _____.
5. Almost none of us _____.
6. None of us _____.

Now I can...

- SPEAKING ☐ talk about clothes.
- GRAMMAR ☐ use comparative adjectives.
- LISTENING ☐ understand short transactions about shopping.
- READING ☐ understand short comparative texts.

| SPEAKING | GRAMMAR | LISTENING | READING |
| Describing people | Be like and look like | Describing people | Describing friends |

What's she like?

 Describe your appearance in three words.

Vocabulary

1 Look at the people. Describe their appearance. Make sentences using these words.

	tall			long	black	
	medium height			short	blonde	
He's a	short	man	with	curly	red	hair.
She's a	good-looking	woman		straight	dark	
	thin					
	heavy					

 Listen and check your sentences.

2 PAIR WORK. Answer the questions. Use the personality words in the box.

| confident | cool | friendly | funny | patient |
| quiet | serious | shy | smart | |

1. What's the actor like?
2. What's the actress like?
3. What's the reporter like?
4. What's the cameraman like?

50

What's she like? • Unit 8

Conversation

1 Complete the conversation. Then listen and check your answers.

a. dark   b. cool   c. actor   d. tall

Clare   Hey! That's Bo Marshall!
Doug   Who?
Clare   Bo Marshall, the [1 c]. He's on this show.
Doug   Which one is he? What does he look like?
Clare   He's [2 d], and he has [3 a] hair.
Doug   Oh, I see him. Do you know him?
Clare   Yes, I do. I was in high school with him.
Doug   Really? What's he like?
Clare   He's really nice. And he's very [4 b].
Doug   I see. Was he your boyfriend in high school?
Clare   I wish!

Now practice the conversation with a partner.

2 PAIR WORK. Practice the conversation again. Use the ideas below. Add your own ideas.

movie star	thin	black	smart
singer	short	red	funny
_____	_____	_____	_____

EXPRESSING EMOTION
Use a rising tone to express surprise.

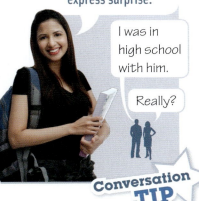

I was in high school with him.

Really?

Conversation TIP

51

What's she like? • Unit 8

Language Practice

Be like and look like
Grammar Reference page 130

What's she **like**?	She's smart, funny, and confident.
What **does** she **look like**?	She's tall and good-looking. She **has** long, curly red hair.
Who **does** she **look like**?	She **looks like** Julia Roberts.

1 Match the questions and answers.

1. What's your sister like? _d_
2. What does your sister look like? ___
3. Who does your sister look like? ___
4. What is your brother like? ___
5. Who does your brother look like? ___

a. He's very smart.
b. She's tall and thin.
c. He looks like me.
d. She's very nice.
e. Nicole Kidman.

2 Complete the conversations.

1. A Do you know my friend Joe Snow?
   B No. _What does he look like_?
   A He's very tall.

2. A Do you know any TV stars?
   B Yes, I do. I know Oprah Winfrey.
   A Really? _____?
   B She's very smart.

3. A Do you know Fred and Betty?
   B No, _____?
   A He's tall, and she's very short.

4. A Do you know anybody famous?
   B Yes. I know Yoko Ono and her son.
   A Really? _____?
   B They're very cool.

3 PAIR WORK. Ask and answer questions like in Activity 2.

> Do you know my friend Carlos Rodriguez?

> No, what does he look like?

Pronunciation—Linked sounds with does and is

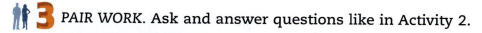

1 Listen. Notice the linked sounds with *does* and *is*.

1. What‿does‿he do?
2. What‿is‿he like?
3. What‿does‿she look like?
4. What‿is‿she doing?

2 Listen again and repeat. Be sure to link the words.

What's she like? • Unit 8

Listening

BEFORE YOU LISTEN Look at the people. What do you think they are like?

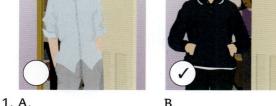

1. A.   B.   2. A.   B.

3. A.   B.   4. A.   B.

CD2 Track 13

1 Listen to the conversations. Check (✓) the correct picture.

◀◀ LISTEN AGAIN. Who is talking? Circle the correct answer.

1. a. two people at a party
   b. a brother and a sister
   c. two people in an online chat room

2. a. a father and a sales clerk
   b. a father and his daughter
   c. a girl and a woman in a store

3. a. two roommates
   b. people thinking about being roommates
   c. a student and a teacher

4. a. two famous baseball players
   b. two friends from English class
   c. a famous baseball player and a fan

CD2 Track 14

2 Listening PLUS Listen to more of the first conversation. Circle the correct answer.

1. John was at college with Alex and ___.
   a. knows of his sister Tina   b. knows of all his sisters

2. Alex has three sisters, and one of them ___.
   a. works in television   b. is a famous movie star

3. Alex's sisters Sandy and Amanda ___.
   a. are both teachers   b. are both college teachers

Smart TALK *My best friend*

Student A: Turn to page 91.
Student B: Turn to page 103.

53

What's she like? • Unit 8

Reading

BEFORE YOU READ Look at the title. What do you think the article is about?

My Best Friend and Me

My best friend is Barbara. She's tall, **slim**, and very pretty. She has long, curly brown hair. I like her because she's a friend when times are good or bad. She's always there when I need her. She's patient, she's **kind**, and she's very **stylish**.

My best friend's name is Diane Costello. She's medium height, and she has straight blonde hair—I want hair like that! I love her because she's a **good listener**, and she understands me. My other friends understand me, but they don't listen!

Pablo Montana is my best friend. He's a year older (I'm 18), but we're in the same college class. We like the same things—soccer, basketball, social network sites. He's tall, and he has short brown hair and a great smile. He's confident, smart, and very cool.

My best friend's name is Lenny Mason. He's a really nice guy. He's tall (but I'm taller!), and he has short blonde hair. He's a very funny guy, and he always looks very **cheerful**. We laugh a lot when we're together. I like my other friends but some of them don't have our **sense of humor**.

ONLINE PRACTICE

1 Read the article. Look at the pictures. Who is Barbara, Diane, Pablo, and Lenny?

2 Read the article again. Circle the correct answer.

1. Why does Diane like Barbara?
   a. She's a friend in bad times.   b. She always needs her.

2. Why does Barbara like Diane?
   a. She listens.   b. Her hair is nice.

3. What things are the same about Pablo and Lenny?
   a. Their age.   b. Their interests.

4. What is different about Pablo and Lenny?
   a. Their sense of humor.   b. Their height.

3 GROUP WORK. Do you know anyone like the four people?

> My friend Luis is like Pablo. He has curly blonde hair.

> Really? My friend Kate has curly blonde hair, too.

Writing Turn to page 111

54

What's she like? • Unit 8

Conversation PLUS —*What kind of person are you?*

1 What kind of person are you? Take the personality quiz.

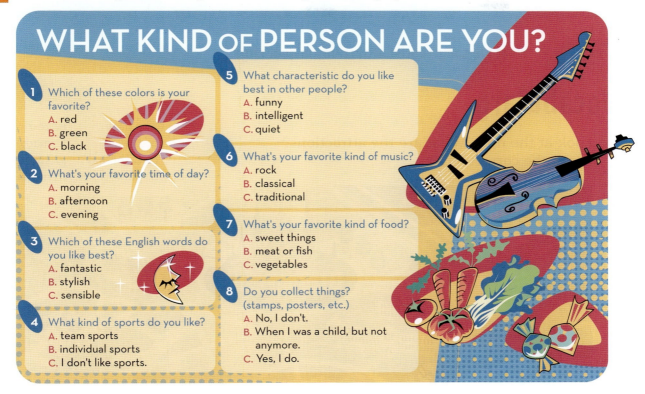

WHAT KIND OF PERSON ARE YOU?

1. Which of these colors is your favorite?
   A. red
   B. green
   C. black

2. What's your favorite time of day?
   A. morning
   B. afternoon
   C. evening

3. Which of these English words do you like best?
   A. fantastic
   B. stylish
   C. sensible

4. What kind of sports do you like?
   A. team sports
   B. individual sports
   C. I don't like sports.

5. What characteristic do you like best in other people?
   A. funny
   B. intelligent
   C. quiet

6. What's your favorite kind of music?
   A. rock
   B. classical
   C. traditional

7. What's your favorite kind of food?
   A. sweet things
   B. meat or fish
   C. vegetables

8. Do you collect things? (stamps, posters, etc.)
   A. No, I don't.
   B. When I was a child, but not anymore.
   C. Yes, I do.

2 GROUP WORK. Use the information below to compare your scores. Who in the class is like you?

20-24 POINTS	15-20 POINTS	10-15 POINTS	0-10 POINTS
You're a good team person. You like working with other people. You also like spending some time alone—but not too much!	You have a lot of energy. You like being with other noisy, lively people. You enjoy having a good time with loud music and good food.	You enjoy being with other people, but only some of the time. Your friends are intelligent and interesting. You don't like too much noise and bright colors.	You prefer being on your own and doing things your own way. You like serious things and are not interested in pop music and sports.
You are: **Sociable**	You are: **lively**	You are: **COOL**	You are: **INDEPENDENT**

SCORE: 3 points for every A answer   2 points for every B answer   1 point for every C answer

3 GROUP WORK. Discuss the results. Do you agree with the description of your personality?

A It's correct. I'm sociable. I like being with people.
B It's completely wrong! I don't like being on my own.

Now I can...

- SPEAKING ☐ describe people's appearances and personalities.
- GRAMMAR ☐ use *be like* and *look like* for descriptions.
- LISTENING ☐ understand short descriptions of people.
- READING ☐ understand short descriptions of friends.

| SPEAKING | GRAMMAR | LISTENING | READING |
| Tourist sites | Can and can't | Describing attractions | Famous cities |

What can you do there?

 What are some tourist attractions in your city?

Vocabulary

1 Look at the map. What are the attractions? Write the correct letter.

a. palace   e. zoo
b. tower   f. market
c. cathedral g. statue
d. park   h. museum

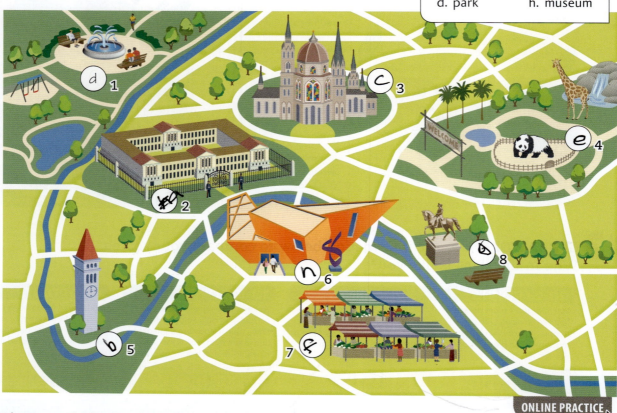

1. d
2. h
3. c
4. e
5. b
6. a
7. f
8. g

 Listen and check your answers.

2 PAIR WORK. Which places do you want to visit? Tell your partner.

A I want to visit the zoo because I love animals.
B I love food, so I want to visit the market.

Connect words with people you know. Make sentences.

Park: Ya-ting goes to a park every week.
Museum: My dad works at a museum.

Vocabulary TIP

56

tourist

What can you do there? • Unit 9

Conversation

 1 Complete the conversation. Then listen and check your answers.

> a. the Zona Rosa   b. Mexico City   c. visit the museums   d. next month

Alex   Guess what? I'm going to visit 1 b .
Marco   Really? I went there last year! When are you going?
Alex   2 d .
Marco   Are you excited?
Alex   Very! Can you tell me some things to see and do there?
Marco   Sure. I always like to 3 c .
Alex   And what about shopping? Where can I go?
Marco   Oh! You can go to 4 a . You can buy a lot of cool things there.
Alex   Thanks!

Now practice the conversation with a partner.

 2 PAIR WORK. Practice the conversation again. Use the ideas below. Add your own ideas.

New York	tomorrow	see the Statue of Liberty	Soho
London	in the summer	walk in Hyde park	Borough Market
_____	_____	_____	_____

57

What can you do there? • Unit 9

Language Practice

Can and can't	Grammar Reference page 131
Where **can** I **go** in Mexico City?	You **can go** to the Zona Rosa.
What **can** I **do** there?	You **can buy** cool things.
What else **can** I **do** there?	You **can eat** good food.
Can I **buy** interesting things there?	Yes, you **can**. No, you **can't**.

1 Complete the questions. Use the verbs in the box.

| buy | eat | take | meet | watch |

1. Where __can__ I __take__ a tour of the city?
2. Where __can__ I __watch__ a good soccer game?
3. Where __can__ I __buy__ some presents?
4. Where __can__ we __eat__ some good food?
5. Where __can__ you __meet__ some interesting people?

2 Complete the conversation.

A Where ___can I look at___ some paintings around here?
B You ___can go___ to the National Gallery.
A When ___can I go___ there?
B You ___can go___ there on weekends.

3 PAIR WORK. Ask and answer the questions in Activity 1.

A Where can I <u>take a tour of the city</u>?
B You can <u>take a tour from a bus downtown</u>.
A When can I <u>take it</u>?
B You can <u>take a tour every day</u>.

Useful Words
every day
on weekends
on Saturdays
on Saturday nights
on Sunday afternoons

Pronunciation—Reduced and unreduced *can* and *can't*

1 Listen. Notice the reduced sound of *can* in statements and questions but not in short answers. *Can't* is never reduced.

1. Can I get there by train?   /kən/ I get there by train?
2. Yes, you can.   Yes you /kæn/.
3. No, you can't.   No, you /kænt/.
4. What can I do there?   What /kən/ can I do there?
5. You can shop and buy gifts.   You /kən/ shop and buy gifts.

2 Listen again and repeat. Be sure to reduce *can* correctly.

58

Listening

BEFORE YOU LISTEN Look at the cities. What do you know about them? What can you do there?

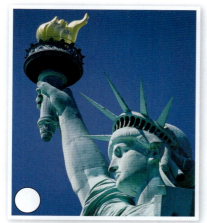
New York City

Rio de Janeiro

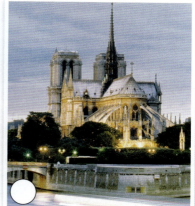
Paris

1 Listen to people talking about their cities. Where do they live? Number the pictures.

⏪ **LISTEN AGAIN.** What is each person's top recommendation? Circle the correct answer.

1. Tomas says ___.
   a. visit museums
   b. listen to music
   c. go shopping
2. Gary says ___.
   a. look at statues
   b. look at buildings
   c. go to Greenwich Village
3. Henri says ___.
   a. visit Notre Dame
   b. walk around
   c. spend time on the river

2 Listening PLUS Listen to the people talk about another city. Check (✓) the things they talk about.

	nightlife	food	music	port	beaches
Fortaleza	✓				
New Orleans					
Marseilles					

3 GROUP WORK. Which city do you want to visit? Why?

I want to visit New Orleans because I like jazz. How about you?

I want to visit Marseilles because I love interesting food!

 *Don't miss it!*

Student A: Turn to page 92.
Student B: Turn to page 104.

What can you do there? • Unit 9

Reading

BEFORE YOU READ Look at the pictures. What do you know about Italy?

CD2 Track 22

VISIT ROME—THE ETERNAL CITY

Rome is the **capital** of Italy. It's located on the west **coast** of the country, about 20 kilometers from the sea. The weather is mild, and it is often sunny. It's one of Europe's most beautiful and interesting cities.

Rome is full of history. You can see **churches** and beautiful palaces that are hundreds of years old. You can also visit the **ruins** of buildings from the **ancient** Roman Empire that are thousands of years old. But Rome is also a busy modern city—and the restaurants are **sensational**! In Rome you can enjoy the architecture, the sunshine, *and* the food.

The historic center of Rome is quite small. You can see the Colosseum, the Pantheon, the Forum, the Spanish Steps, and the Vatican—all in one day! That's great if you really want to see everything quickly.

But why hurry? Take your time! Then you can see—and enjoy—one of the world's great cities.

THE COLOSSEUM

THE FORUM

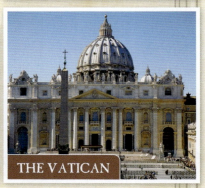
THE VATICAN

1 Read the article. Which places in Rome do you want to visit?

2 Read the article again. Answer the questions.
1. How far is Rome from the sea?
2. What is the weather like?
3. What are the restaurants like?
4. What is the historic center of the city like?

3 CLASS ACTIVITY. What can you see in your city?

> In the city, you can go to many theaters and museums.

> And in the city center, you can go to the opera house.

Writing Turn to page 112

60

What can you do there? • Unit 9

Conversation PLUS —Come visit!

1 Look at the advertisement for New Zealand. What can you do there?

2 PAIR WORK. Choose a place you know (city, region, or country). Answer the questions.

1. What are some interesting places you can visit there? _____.
2. What sports and activities can you do …
   in the spring? _____
   in the summer? _____
   in the fall? _____
   in the winter? _____
3. What foods can you eat there? Where can you eat them? _____
4. What are some good souvenirs? Where can you buy them? _____

3 GROUP WORK. Tell your group about the place. Use the information in Activity 2.

My place is Costa Rica. You can do a lot of great things there! You can visit great beaches, and you can…

Now I can...

- SPEAKING ☐ talk about tourist sites.
- GRAMMAR ☐ use *can* and *can't*.
- LISTENING ☐ understand descriptions of city attractions.
- READING ☐ understand short texts about famous cities.

Review Units 7-9

1 Read the conversation. Circle the correct answer.

Reporter	Excuse me, I'm from WFBN Radio. Your clothes are fantastic. You <u>look / look like</u> a movie star!
Woman	Oh, thank you.
Reporter	Can you tell the listeners about them?
Woman	OK. I'm wearing a baggy white jacket, a black T-shirt, and jeans. [SAY MORE]
Reporter	Tell me about your jacket. [SAY MORE]
Woman	It's a man's jacket.
Reporter	Really? Do you like men's jackets?
Woman	Yes. They're more comfortable <u>than / as</u> women's jackets.
Reporter	I see. And are they cheaper?
Woman	No. This is <u>more expensive / as expensive as</u> a woman's jacket.
Reporter	And your jeans… Are they designer jeans?
Woman	No, they're regular jeans. They're <u>better / good</u> than designer jeans.
Reporter	I see. And you're wearing high heels.
Woman	That's right. [SAY MORE]
Reporter	They <u>look / look like</u> great!
Woman	Thanks!

 Listen and check your answers. Then practice the conversation with a partner.

2 PAIR WORK. Put a box around the clothes. Practice the conversation again. Use your own ideas for the clothes.

3 Practice the conversation again. This time add information and [SAY MORE].

Reporter	Can you tell the listeners about them?
Woman	OK. I'm wearing a baggy white jacket, a black T-shirt, and jeans. [I'm also wearing a scarf.]

Review • Units 7-9

4 Look at the website. What kind of website do you think it is?

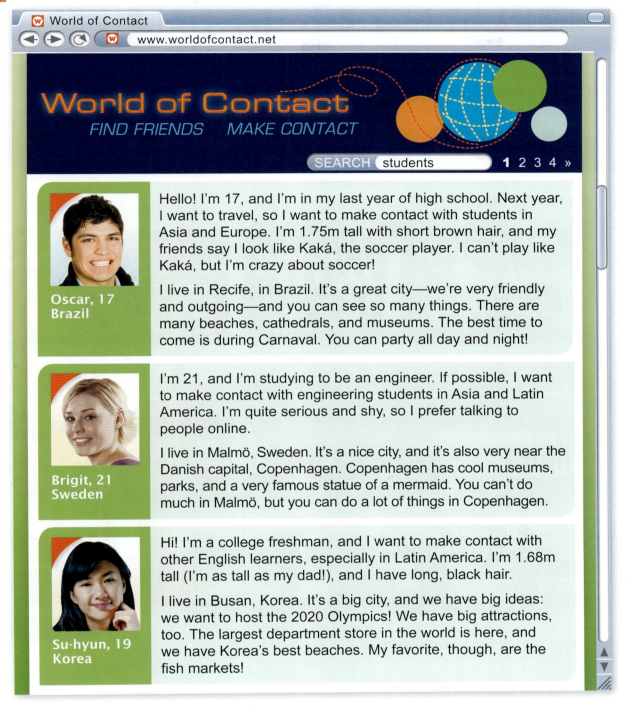

5 Read the introductions. Answer the questions.

1. Who describes his/her appearance?
2. Who describes his/her personality?
3. Which hometown is near a capital city?
4. Which hometown wants to host the Olympics?
5. Which hometown is a good place to swim?

6 GROUP WORK. Write something about you for the website. Then share it with your group.

10 Is there a bank near here?

SPEAKING	GRAMMAR	LISTENING	READING
Places around town	*There is* and *there are*	Tourist facilities	Favorite places

 Warm UP What is your favorite place in your neighborhood?

Vocabulary

1 Look at the picture. What's in the mall? Write the correct letter.

- a. coffee shop
- b. shoe store
- c. convenience store
- d. department store
- e. cheap restaurant
- f. Internet cafe
- g. movie theater
- h. bookstore
- i. bank

1. i
2. e
3. g
4. b
5. d
6. a
7. c
8. h
9. g

CD2 Track 25 Listen and check your answers.

2 Match the places and the things you can do there.

1. a bank __f__
2. a bookstore __d__
3. an Internet cafe __a__
4. a coffee shop __b__
5. a department store __c__
6. a convenience store __e__

a. check your e-mail
b. have coffee
c. try on a pair of jeans
d. buy a dictionary
e. look at magazines
f. change money

3 PAIR WORK. What other things can you do at these places? Tell you partner.

A What can you buy at a convenience store?
B You can buy snacks, drinks, and magazines.

64

Is there a bank near here? • Unit 10

Conversation

1 Complete the conversation. Then listen and check your answers.

> a. restaurants   b. get something to eat   c. a bank   d. change some money

Brian   Hi. Can you help me?
Ana   Sure. What can I do for you?
Brian   I want to 1 __d__ . Is there 2 __c__ in the neighborhood?
Ana   Yes, there is. There's one across the street.
Brian   Across the street?
Ana   Yes.
Brian   OK, and I'd like to 3 __b__ . Are there any 4 _____ around here?
Ana   No, sorry, there aren't. But there are some downtown.
Brian   Great. Thanks!
Ana   You're welcome.

Now practice the conversation with a partner.

2 PAIR WORK. Practice the conversation again. Use the ideas below. Add your own ideas.

send an e-mail	an Internet cafe	buy some shoes	shoe stores
buy a dictionary	a bookstore	watch a movie	movie theaters

CONFIRMING INFORMATION
Use echo questions to check your understanding

There's one across the street.

Across the street?

Conversation TIP

Is there a bank near here? • Unit 10

Language Practice

There is and **there are** — Grammar Reference page 132

There's a bank next door.
There isn't a bank around here.
Is there a bank in the neighborhood? Yes, **there is. There's one** across the street.
  No, **there isn't.**

There are some bookstores downtown.
There aren't any bookstores around here.
Are there any bookstores around here? Yes, **there are.** No, **there aren't.**

ONLINE PRACTICE

1 Complete the sentences.

1. I'm very happy because __there's__ a movie theater in my neighborhood.
2. __There is__ a gym around here, but __there are__ a nice park across the street.
3. I'm unhappy because __There are__ any cheap restaurants in my neighborhood.
4. __there is__ a coffee shop across the street, but __There are__ any Internet cafes.

2 Complete the questions.

1. __Is there__ a post office near you?
2. __is there__ a train station in your neighborhood?
3. __are there__ any shopping malls in your town?
4. __are there__ any convenience stores in your neighborhood?

Useful Words
across the street
around the corner
across from my house
near my house
down the street
on my street
ten minutes away
on the next block

3 PAIR WORK. Ask and answer the questions in Activity 2. Use information about your neighborhood or town.

A Is there a post office near you?
B Yes, there is. It's across the street.
   No, there isn't. But there is one near the train station.

Pronunciation—Word stress in compound nouns

1 Listen. Notice the word in a compound noun that gets more stress.

1. I like to go to the **coffee** shop.
2. My father works in a **department** store.
3. The **train** station isn't far from here.
4. Is there a **movie** theater in your town?

2 Listen again and repeat. Be sure to stress the correct word.

66

Listening

BEFORE YOU LISTEN Look at the picture. Where do you think the man wants to go?

1 Listen to the woman helping tourists. Where do they want to go? Write 1–4.

___ coffee shop   ___ park
_1_ swimming pool   ___ shoe stores
___ hotel   ___ Internet cafe

◀◀ LISTEN AGAIN. Match the places with their locations.

1. swimming pool ___   a. on the next block
2. park ___   b. on Market Street
3. shoe stores ___   c. around the corner
4. coffee shop ___   d. two blocks away

2 Listening PLUS Listen to the tourists later. Check (✓) the things that are a problem.

☐ The outdoor swimming pool.
☐ The walk to downtown.
☐ The cost of using a computer at the business center.
☐ The price of a taxi downtown.

 *Is there a bank?*

Student A: Turn to page 93.
Student B: Turn to page 105.

Is there a bank near here? • Unit 10

Reading

BEFORE YOU READ Look at the pictures. What do you think you can do in these cities?

CD2
Track 31

Having fun downtown

Hi, my name is Brian Burns, and I come from Australia. I live in Sydney. It's a great place to visit—great beaches, great weather, and great for outdoor sports. There are also **clubs**, movie theaters, and a lot of free entertainment in the streets and parks.

My favorite part of Sydney is Chinatown. It's so lively! There are many cheap restaurants and **grocery stores**, and there are department stores where you can find interesting Chinese clothing. Every year, there's a big celebration of Chinese New Year. It's so fun and colorful! I go every year.

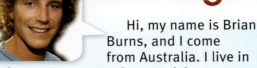

Hello, my name is Sarah Chan, and I live in Vancouver, Canada—the greatest city in the world! Vancouver has everything. In the spring, you can ski in the mountains and swim in the ocean—on the same day! Really! And Vancouver is a great place to walk. There are some terrific outdoor **markets** and **plazas**. They are nice places to spend a sunny afternoon.

Yaletown is my favorite neighborhood. There are a lot of coffee shops, **furniture stores**, bookstores, and **boutiques**. On weekends, I go with my friends and hang out all day. At night, we often go to a movie theater and watch the latest movie—and rest our feet!

Sydney

Vancouver

ONLINE PRACTICE

1 Read the article. Check (✓) the things Brian and Sarah talk about.

	movie theaters	restaurants	coffee shops	bookstores	department stores
Brian					
Sarah					

2 Read the article again. Answer the questions.

1. Why is Sydney a good place to be outdoors?
2. What kinds of stores are in Chinatown?
3. What can you do in Vancouver in the spring?
4. Why does Sarah like Yaletown?

3 PAIR WORK. Compare your neighborhood with Chinatown and Yaletown.

> In my neighborhood, there are coffee shops, but there isn't a theater.

> In mine, there are many restaurants, but there aren't any bookstores.

Writing
Turn to page 112

68

Is there a bank near here? • Unit 10

Conversation PLUS —*Your favorite places*

1 Look at the questions in the survey. Add a question. Then write your answers.

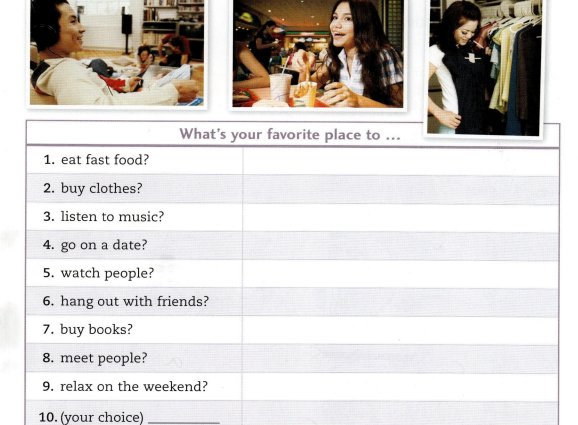

What's your favorite place to …	
1. eat fast food?	
2. buy clothes?	
3. listen to music?	
4. go on a date?	
5. watch people?	
6. hang out with friends?	
7. buy books?	
8. meet people?	
9. relax on the weekend?	
10. (your choice) _____	

2 GROUP WORK. Tell each other about your favorite places. Ask questions and try to give extra information!

My favorite place to buy clothes is the mall.

Why do you like it?

Where is it?

3 CLASS ACTIVITY. Share your information with the class.

The Bongo Room is my favorite place to listen to music. It's always open late, and it has live bands every weekend. It's near the…

Now I can...

- **SPEAKING** ☐ talk about places around town.
- **GRAMMAR** ☐ use *there is* and *there are*.
- **LISTENING** ☐ understand exchanges about tourist facilities.
- **READING** ☐ understand short texts about favorite places.

11 Did you have a good time?

SPEAKING	GRAMMAR	LISTENING	READING
Vacation activities	Simple past	Describing vacations	Hotel description

 Do you go on vacation? Where do you go?

Vocabulary

1 Look at the picture. What happened? Write the correct letter.

- a. sit on the beach
- b. forget your passport
- c. miss your plane
- d. visit an art gallery
- e. climb a mountain
- f. lose your luggage
- g. write postcards
- h. break your arm

 Listen and check your answers.

2 PAIR WORK. Ask and answer questions about vacations.

A What do you do on vacation?
B I sometimes <u>visit a museum</u>. What about you?
A I always <u>sit on the beach</u>.
B I never <u>write postcards</u>.

Make word associations to learn new words.

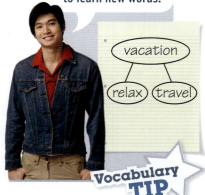

Vocabulary TIP

70

Did you have a good time? • Unit 11

Conversation

1 Complete the conversation. Then listen and check your answers.

a. sister   b. Hawaii   c. on the beach   d. a great restaurant

Kelly   You look great!
Emily   Thanks. I was on vacation last week.
Kelly   Where did you go?
Emily   I went to 1 [b] with my 2 [a].
Kelly   Wow! Did you have a good time?
Emily   We had an awesome time. It's a great place! We spent every day 3 [c], and every night we went to 4 [d].
Kelly   And did you meet anyone interesting?
Emily   Yes, I did.
Kelly   Really? Tell me more!
Emily   No! It's a secret!

Now practice the conversation with a partner.

2 PAIR WORK. Practice the conversation again. Use the ideas below. Add your own ideas.

Chicago	mom and dad	in the city	a musical
Colorado	friends	in the mountains	a show
_____	_____	_____	_____

71

Did you have a good time? • Unit 11

Language Practice

CD2 ›)
Track 34

The simple past	Grammar Reference page 133
Did you **go** anywhere on vacation?	Yes, I **did.** I **went** to Hawaii. No, I **didn't.** I **stayed** home.
What **did** you **do?** Where **did** you **stay?** Who **did** you **go** with?	I **went** to the beach. I **stayed** in a nice hotel. I **went** with my sister

ONLINE PRACTICE

1 Complete the sentences. Use the verbs in the box.

> go   lose   meet   make   take   write   visit

1. I ____met____ an interesting guy from Brazil last week.
2. I __write__ a lot of postcards at the hotel.
3. We __visited__ to Taipei last summer. It was fantastic!
4. The airline __med__ a mistake, and I __lost__ my luggage.
5. We _____ galleries, and I _____ photos with my new camera.

2 Complete the questions. Then answer them with information about you.

1. A Where _____did you go_____ on your last vacation?
   B I went to blrte

2. A How long __did you__ there?
   B _____.

3. A Where did you stay?
   B in hotil .

4. A did you do anything interesting?
   B _____.

Regular verbs	
arrive → arrived	
miss → missed	
visit → visited	

Irregular verbs	
go → went	see → saw
lose → lost	take → took
make → made	write → wrote

3 PAIR WORK. Ask and answer the questions in Activity 2.

Pronunciation—*Reduction of* did you

CD2 ›)
Track 35

1 Listen. Notice the reduced sounds of *did you*.

Unreduced	Reduced
1. Did you go on vacation?	*Diju* go on vacation?
2. What did you do?	*Whadiju* do?
3. Where did you stay?	Where *diju* stay?
4. How did you get there?	How *diju* get there?

2 Listen again and repeat. Be sure to say the reduced sounds.

72

Did you have a good time? • Unit 11

Listening

BEFORE YOU LISTEN Look at the cities. Where are they? What do you know about them?

Acapulco

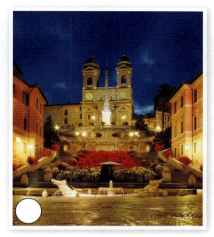
Rome

Hong Kong

1 Listen to people talking about their vacations. Where did they go? Number the pictures.

◀◀ LISTEN AGAIN. Complete the chart.

	What went wrong?	Who did they meet?	What did they like best?
1.			The people
2.	The airline lost her luggage		
3.		Some Spanish people	

2 Listening PLUS Listen to more of Brian's conversation. Put the events in the correct order.

1. He went to the police station in Acapulco. _1_
2. He got a message from the Acapulco police. ___
3. He visited the Canadian consulate. ___
4. He flew to Acapulco. ___
5. The hotel in Acapulco called him. ___
6. He flew to Mexico City. ___

 *What did you do there?*

Student A: Turn to page 94.
Student B: Turn to page 106.

73

Did you have a good time? • Unit 11

Reading

BEFORE YOU READ Look at the pictures. What kind of place is this?

CD2 Track 38

A Weekend at the Ice Hotel

About 20 minutes west of Quebec City in Canada, there's a **unique** place—the only hotel in North America made **entirely** of ice and snow. We sent Sandy Russell to find out more…

When I arrived, it was **freezing**. The outside temperature was -28°C! I thought, "Do I *really* want to sleep in a hotel made of *ice*?"

But when I walked inside, I was **astounded**. It was warmer than outside—about -4°. This is because of the walls. They're 120 centimeters thick. And the hotel was **absolutely** wonderful! The floors and ceilings were ice. There were beautiful ice sculptures everywhere. There were also two art galleries, a movie theater, a skating rink, and a wedding chapel. Even the drinking glasses were made of ice! And in the rooms? Yes, the beds were made of ice. I slept in a **cozy** sleeping bag on a mattress, and the mattress was on top of deer skins. It was a lot of fun!

They build the ice hotel every year in December, and you can stay there from January to March. In past years, more than 4,000 guests stayed at least one night.

Beaches, mountains, lakes, museums—boring! The place to go is the ice hotel.

ONLINE PRACTICE

1 Read the article. Answer the questions.

1. Where is the ice hotel?
2. What was the difference between the temperature outside the hotel and inside?
3. What can you do at the ice hotel?
4. How long is the ice hotel open?
5. How many people went to see the ice hotel in past years?

2 CLASS ACTIVITY. Did you ever visit an unusual place?

Last summer, I went to an eco-hotel in the mountains. It was very interesting because…

Writing
Turn to page 113

Did you have a good time? • Unit 11

Conversation PLUS —*Your best vacation*

1 Look at the questions in the survey. Add a question. Then write your answers.

	You	Student 1	Student 2
1. When was your best vacation?			
2. Where did you go?			
3. Who did you go with?			
4. How long were you there?			
5. What activities did you do?			
6. What souvenirs did you buy?			
7. What did you eat and drink?			
8. Did you meet anyone interesting?			
9. Why was it your best vacation?			
10. (your choice) _____			

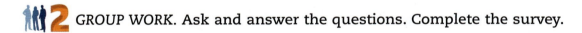

2 GROUP WORK. Ask and answer the questions. Complete the survey.

3 GROUP WORK. Ask more questions. Try to give extra information!

> My best vacation was in Chile.

> Do you want to go again?

> Did you try something new?

Now I can...

- **SPEAKING** ☐ talk about vacation activities.
- **GRAMMAR** ☐ use the simple past.
- **LISTENING** ☐ understand short descriptions of vacations.
- **READING** ☐ understand a description of a hotel.

SPEAKING	GRAMMAR	LISTENING	READING
Future plans	Going to + verb	Travel plans	Travel blog

12 I'm going to go by car.

Warm UP What kinds of transportation do you use often?

Vocabulary

1 Look at the picture. What kinds of transportation are there? Write the correct letter.

a. sports car f. train
b. helicopter g. SUV
c. limousine   h. truck
d. motorcycle i. van
e. plane

 Listen and check your answers.

2 PAIR WORK. Ask and answer questions about transportation.

How do you get to class?

I usually take a bus.

Useful Words
Go by train/bus/taxi/car/subway/plane
Go on foot

Take a train/bus/taxi/subway
Drive a car/truck/van
Ride a bicycle/motorcycle

76

transportation.

I'm going to go by car. • Unit 12

Conversation

1 Complete the conversation. Then listen and check your answers.

a. five days   b. plane   c. Rome   d. aunt and uncle

Ana   Hey! No classes next week! What are you going to do?
Anthony I'm going to visit my [1_____].
Ana   Where do they live?
Anthony They live in [2_____].
Ana   Wow! That's far. How are you going to get there?
Anthony I'm going to go by [3_____]. I just bought my ticket.
Ana   How long are you going to stay?
Anthony I'm going to stay for [4_____], maybe a little longer.
Ana   And what are you going to do?
Anthony Nothing! I'm going to chill out!

Now practice the conversation with a partner.

GIVING MORE INFORMATION
When you answer a question, give more details.

2 PAIR WORK. Practice the conversation again. Use the ideas below. Add your own ideas.

grandparents	Buenos Aires	train	two days
best friends	South Africa	bus	a week
_____	_____	_____	_____

How are you going to get there?

By plane. I just bought my ticket.

Conversation TIP

77

I'm going to go by car. • Unit 12

Language Practice

Going to + verb　　　　　　　　　　　　　　　　　　　　Grammar Reference page 134

| Are you **going to go** by train? | Yes, I **am**. | No, I**'m not**. |
| Is she **going to ride** a motorcycle? | Yes, she **is**. | No, she **isn't**. |

What **are** you **going to do**?　　　I**'m going to see** my friends.
How **are** you **going to get** there?　I**'m going to take** a bus.
How long **are** you **going to stay**?　I**'m going to stay** for two days.

1 Check (✓) the sentences if they are true for you.
If not, rewrite them so they are.

1. I'm going to stay home tonight. ☐
   _____

2. I'm going to see my family this weekend. ☐
   _____

3. I'm going to take a bus after class. ☐
   _____

4. I'm not going to take the subway tomorrow. ☐
   _____

5. I'm not going to take a plane next summer. ☐
   _____

2 Match the questions and answers.

1. Where are you going on your next vacation? _e_
2. When are you going to go? ___
3. How are you going to get there? ___
4. How long are you going to stay there? ___
5. What are you going to do? ___

a. Maybe June or July.
b. About two weeks.
c. I'm going to go to the beach!
d. I'm going to go by plane.
e. Florida, probably.

Pronunciation—*Reduction of* going to

1 Listen. Notice the reduced sound of *going to*.

Unreduced	Reduced
1. What are you going to do?	What are you *gonna* do?
2. Is she going to be a doctor?	Is she *gonna* be a doctor?
3. He's going to study tonight.	He's *gonna* study tonight.
4. They're going to watch a DVD.	They're *gonna* watch a DVD.

2 Listen again and repeat. Be sure to say the reduced sound.

I'm going to go by car. • Unit 12

Listening

BEFORE YOU LISTEN Look at the pictures. Where do you want to go on vacation?

New York City

Appalachian Mountains

Hawaii

1 Listen to the people. Where do they usually go on vacation? Number the pictures.

◀◀ LISTEN AGAIN. Complete the chart.

	Where are they going to go this year?	How are they going to get there?	How do they feel about it?
Steve			really excited
Jennifer		by train	
Hank	Europe		

2 Listening PLUS Listen to the people later. Circle the correct answer.

1. Is Steve going to travel non-stop to his destination?
   a. Yes, he is.
   b. No, he's going to go sightseeing.
   c. No, he's going to spend the night in a motel.

2. Why is Jennifer excited?
   a. It's her first time on a train.
   b. She's going to do some sightseeing.
   c. They're going to sleep on the train.

3. Why is Hank not happy?
   a. He doesn't like traveling by plane.
   b. He's waiting a long time in the departure lounge.
   c. He's going to arrive in London late at night.

 *Where are they going to go?*

Student A: Turn to page 95.
Student B: Turn to page 107.

I'm going to go by car. • Unit 12

Reading

BEFORE YOU READ Look at the title and pictures. What do you think the blog is about?

CD2 Track 45

Tom and Judy's Travel Blog

Our Australian Adventure—Day 15: Alice Springs

Hi, everyone! We're in Alice Springs, right in the middle of the country. We're very excited because today we're going to see one of the most amazing *races* in the world—the World Solar Challenge!

It's a 3,000 km *long-distance* car race from Darwin in the north to Adelaide in the south (see the map for the *route*), and all the cars are *solar powered*! We're going to take a look because, well, we want to drive a car like that in the future.

The first WSC race was in 1987, and now it usually takes place every two years. There are teams from many different countries. Some of them are high school teams! It's super cool, and it's *eco-friendly*. In fact, we're thinking about building a solar-powered car and bringing it back next time!

After this, Tom and I are *heading* west to Perth. Unfortunately, we're not going to drive a solar-powered car. We're going to take the train.

We're going to write our next blog in the capital of Western Australia. Talk soon!

solar-powered car

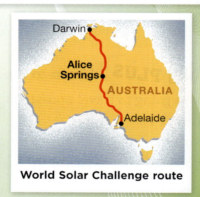
World Solar Challenge route

ONLINE PRACTICE

1 Read the blog. Answer the questions.

1. Where is Alice Springs?
2. What is special about the cars in the race?
3. How long is the race?
4. Where are Tom and Judy going to go next?
5. Are they going to drive there?
6. How are they going to get there?

2 CLASS ACTIVITY. In the future, do you think people are going to drive solar-powered cars? Why?

I think people are going to drive solar-powered cars because…

Writing
Turn to page 113

I'm going to go by car. • Unit 12

Conversation PLUS —*How are you going to get there?*

1 Look at the pictures. Which transportation do you like? Which ones do you not like? Why?

Where are you going to go …	You	How	Your partner	How
after school?				
tomorrow?				
this weekend?				
next summer?				
(your choice) _____				
(your choice) _____				

2 Look at the questions in the survey. Add two more questions. Then write your answers.

3 PAIR WORK. Ask and answer the questions. Complete the survey.

4 GROUP WORK. Compare your answers. How "green" are your travel plans? Are you going to change them?

> After school, I usually take the bus home. I'm not going to change my plans. I'm a green traveler!

> I'm going to the mall this weekend. My mom's going to drive. but maybe we can take the subway instead.

Now I can...

- **SPEAKING** ☐ talk about future plans.
- **GRAMMAR** ☐ use *going to* + verb for future plans.
- **LISTENING** ☐ understand short descriptions of travel plans.
- **READING** ☐ understand texts about travel activities.

81

Review Units 10-12

1 Read the conversation. Circle the correct answer.

Teacher	Good night, Larry. See you next week.
Larry	Actually, I'm *going to go / go* on vacation next week to Mexico. [SAY MORE]
	1
Teacher	Really? That's great! How are you going to get there?
Larry	I'm going to take a plane to Mexico City.
Teacher	And what *you are / are you* going to do there?
	2
Larry	I'm going to do some sightseeing and visit art galleries. I *studied / studyed* art in school.
	3
Teacher	I didn't know that.
Larry	I also want to rent a car and drive to some places.
Teacher	Oh, actually, why don't you take a bus to Acapulco or Cancun?
Larry	Are they nice places?
Teacher	Sure! *There's / There are* some great beaches there. You can relax, swim, and sit on the beach. [SAY MORE]
	4
Larry	I'm not really a beach person. [SAY MORE]
Teacher	Really?
Larry	Yeah, and *there are / are there* a lot of tourists in places like that.
	5
Teacher	Is that a problem?
Larry	Yes! I want to practice my Spanish!

Listen and check your answers. Then practice the conversation with a partner.

 2 PAIR WORK. Put a box around the transportation words and vacation activities. Practice the conversation again. Use your own ideas for transportation and activities.

3 Practice the conversation again. This time add information and [SAY MORE].

Larry	I'm *going to go / go* on vacation next week to Mexico. [I'm going for five days.]
	1
Teacher	Really? That's great!

Review • Units 10–12

4 Look at the pictures and read the first sentence. Why do you think the man visited New Orleans?

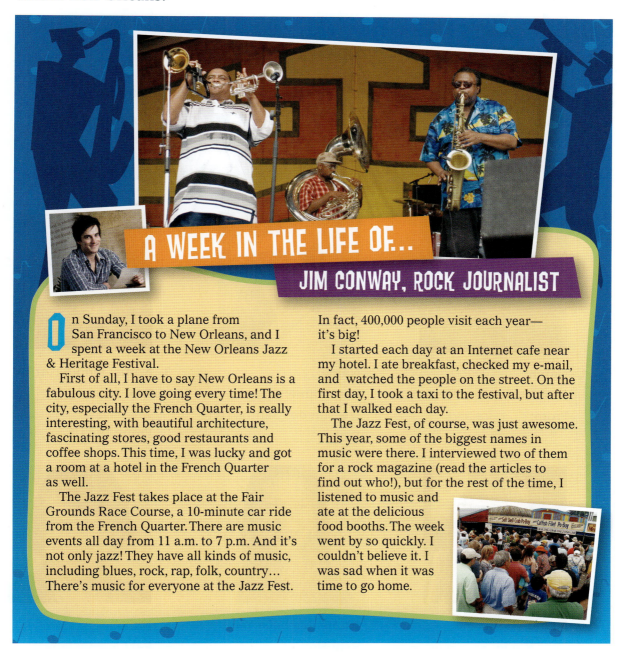

A WEEK IN THE LIFE OF...
JIM CONWAY, ROCK JOURNALIST

On Sunday, I took a plane from San Francisco to New Orleans, and I spent a week at the New Orleans Jazz & Heritage Festival.

First of all, I have to say New Orleans is a fabulous city. I love going every time! The city, especially the French Quarter, is really interesting, with beautiful architecture, fascinating stores, good restaurants and coffee shops. This time, I was lucky and got a room at a hotel in the French Quarter as well.

The Jazz Fest takes place at the Fair Grounds Race Course, a 10-minute car ride from the French Quarter. There are music events all day from 11 a.m. to 7 p.m. And it's not only jazz! They have all kinds of music, including blues, rock, rap, folk, country… There's music for everyone at the Jazz Fest.

In fact, 400,000 people visit each year—it's big!

I started each day at an Internet cafe near my hotel. I ate breakfast, checked my e-mail, and watched the people on the street. On the first day, I took a taxi to the festival, but after that I walked each day.

The Jazz Fest, of course, was just awesome. This year, some of the biggest names in music were there. I interviewed two of them for a rock magazine (read the articles to find out who!), but for the rest of the time, I listened to music and ate at the delicious food booths. The week went by so quickly. I couldn't believe it. I was sad when it was time to go home.

5 Read the article. Check (✓) *True* or *False*.

	True	False
1. This was Jim's first time to New Orleans.	☐	☐
2. The French Quarter is a short car ride from New Orleans.	☐	☐
3. Musicians at the Jazz Fest play many styles of music.	☐	☐
4. Jim walked to the festival every day.	☐	☐
5. Jim is going to write articles for a magazine.	☐	☐
6. Jim had a great time in New Orleans.	☐	☐

6 GROUP WORK. Have you been to a music festival? What is it like? Tell your group.

Smart Talk

Unit 1—Who's that?
Student A

1 PAIR WORK. Ask and answer questions to complete the information.

A Who's <u>number 1</u>?
B That's <u>Bono</u>. What's <u>his</u> real name?
A <u>His</u> real name is <u>Paul Hewson</u>. Where is <u>he</u> from?
B <u>He's</u> from <u>Ireland</u>.

> **Useful Language**
> How do you spell that?
> Can you repeat that?
> Did you say ... ?

1. Name: ____Bono____
   Real Name: Paul Hewson
   From: ____Ireland____

2. Name: _____
   Real Name: Ricardo Izecson dos Santos Leite
   From: _____

3. Name: Jennifer Aniston
   Real Name: _____
   _____
   From: the US

4. Name: _____
   Real Name: Shaquille O'Neal
   From: _____

5. Name: Michelle Yeoh
   Real Name: _____
   _____
   From: Malaysia

6. Name: _____
   Real Name: James Eugene Carrey
   From: _____

2 Ask about your partner's favorite stars. Complete the sentences.

1. My partner's favorite singer is _____.
2. He / She is from _____.
3. My partner's favorite actor is _____.
4. He / She is from _____.
5. My partner's favorite athlete is _____.
6. His / Her real name is _____.

> Who's your favorite...?
> Where's she from?
> What's his real name?

Smart Talk • Student A

Unit 2—What do they do?
Student A

1 PAIR WORK. Look at the pictures. Ask and answer questions to complete the information.

A What <u>does Robin</u> do?
B <u>She's a doctor.</u>
A Where <u>does she</u> work?
B <u>She works</u> in <u>a hospital</u>.

1. Robin
   Job: _doctor_
   Works in: _a hospital_

2. Alan
   Job: teacher
   Works in: a college

3. Jane and Kim
   Job: _____
   Work in: _____

4. Mark and Yuko
   Job: pilots
   Work in: an airport

5. Sang
   Job: _____
   Works in: _____

6. Erika
   Job: architect
   Works in: an office

2 Ask your partner about these people. Write their jobs.

1. My partner is _____.
2. My partner's dad is _____.
3. My partner's mom is _____.
4. My partner's friend is _____.
5. _____ is my partner's dream job.

Useful Words
What does your ___ do?
What's your dream job?

a businessman / businesswoman
a housewife   an office worker
an assistant   between jobs
self-employed

85

Smart Talk • Student A

Unit 3—*Does he like fish?*
Student A

1 PAIR WORK. Ask and answer questions to complete the chart. Ask about the six food items.

A Does Joe <u>love</u> <u>ice cream</u>?
B No, he doesn't.
A Does he <u>love</u> <u>salad</u>?
B No, he doesn't.
A Does he <u>love</u> <u>fish</u>?
B Yes, he does. That's right!

Food

2 Ask and answer questions to complete the sentences.

1. I like _____, but my partner doesn't.
2. I don't like _____, but my partner does.
3. My partner and I both like _____ and _____.
4. We both don't like _____ and _____.
5. We both love _____.

Do you like ___?

I don't like ___. How about you?

I don't like ___ either.

86

Smart Talk • Student A

Unit 4—*How often?*
Student A

 1 PAIR WORK. Ask and answer questions to complete the chart.

A What does <u>Amy</u> do to keep fit?
B She <u>goes swimming</u>.
A How often does she <u>go swimming</u>?
B <u>Twice a week</u>.
A Does she like it?
B <u>Yes, she does</u>. It's fun!

	What do they do to keep fit?	How often?	Do they like it?
Amy	swimming	twice a week	Yes. It's fun!
Chris	jogging	every day	No. It's tiring.
Sara			
Gabriel	go to the gym	four nights a week	Yes. The gym has TVs!
Kim and Max			

2 What does your partner do to keep fit? Complete the sentences.

1. My partner _____ goes to the gym.
2. My partner _____ plays basketball.
3. My partner _____ does yoga.
4. My partner _____ goes swimming.
5. My partner _____ goes bicycling.

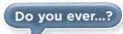

87

Smart Talk • Student A

Unit 5—*What is he doing?*
Student A

1 PAIR WORK. Look at the people. Who are they? Ask and answer questions with a partner. Ask about the names in the box.

A Is <u>Ellen</u> <u>talking on the phone</u>?
B No, she's not.
A Is she <u>checking her e-mail</u>?
B Yes, she is.

Names
Ellen
Michelle
Betsy
Alice

2 What is your partner doing right now? Check (✓) *True* or *False*.

	True	False
1. My partner is sending a text message.	☐	☐
2. My partner is thinking about lunch.	☐	☐
3. My partner is looking at the teacher.	☐	☐
4. My partner is daydreaming.	☐	☐
5. My partner is speaking in English.	☐	☐

Are you ____ right now?

Yes, I am. How about you?

Smart Talk • Student A

Unit 6—*Where were they?*
Student A

 1 PAIR WORK. Look at the people. Where were they on Saturday? Where are they now? Ask and answer questions to complete the information.

A Where <u>was Tom</u> on Saturday?
B <u>He was at a party</u>. Where <u>is he</u> now?
A <u>He's in class</u>.

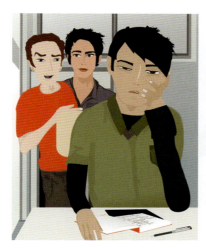

1. Tom
   Saturday: <u>at a party</u>
   Now: in class

2. Miho
   Saturday: _____
   Now: in Paris

3. Amy and Jen
   Saturday: on a mountain
   Now: _____

4. Susan
   Saturday: _____
   Now: at a game

5. Bill and Mary
   Saturday: in the park
   Now: _____

6. Mike
   Saturday: _____
   Now: at home

2 Ask your partner about the people. Where were they on Saturday?

1. My partner was _____ on Saturday.
2. My partner's friend was _____ on Saturday.
3. My partner's brother / sister was _____ on Saturday.
4. My partner's parents were _____ on Saturday.

Where were you...?

Where was your...?

89

Smart Talk • Student A

Unit 7—Which one do you like?
Student A

 1 PAIR WORK. Look at the pictures. Ask and answer questions to complete the information.

A How much <u>are the jeans</u>?
B <u>They're $35</u>. Where are <u>they</u> from?
A <u>They're</u> from <u>the US</u>. What <u>colors</u> do you have?
B <u>Blue, black, or green</u>.

1. Jeans
   Price: <u>$35</u>
   From: the US
   Colors: <u>Blue, black, green</u>

2. Baggy pants
   Price: _____
   From: Japan
   Colors: _____

3. Sweater
   Price: $100
   From: _____
   Sizes: Small, medium

4. Sweatshirt
   Price: _____
   From: China
   Sizes: _____

5. T-shirt
   Price: $20
   From: _____
   Styles: long-sleeved, short-sleeved

6. Shirt
   Price: _____
   From: Italy
   Styles: _____

7. High heels
   Price: $100
   From: _____
   Colors: Black, red, blue

8. Sneakers
   Price: _____
   From: the US
   Colors: _____

2 Compare the clothes in each row. Which do you like? Why?

A Which do you like, the <u>jeans</u> or the <u>baggy pants</u>?
B I like <u>the baggy pants</u>.
A Really? Why?
B I think they're <u>more comfortable</u>. How about you?
A I like the jeans. They're <u>more practical</u>.
   And <u>they're cheaper</u>!

Useful Words

cheap	fashionable
colorful	nice
comfortable	practical
elegant	stylish
expensive	warm

90

Unit 8 — *My best friend*
Student A

1 PAIR WORK. Answer the questions about your best friend. Then compare answers with a partner. Write your partner's answers in the survey.

A What's his or her name?
B It's <u>Maria</u>.
A Where is she from?
B <u>She's</u> from <u>Mexico City</u>.
A When is <u>her</u> birthday?
B <u>I'm not sure</u>.

	My best friend	My partner's best friend
1. What's his / her name?		
2. Where is he / she from?		
3. How old is he / she?		
4. When is his / her birthday?		
5. What's he / she like? (smart, cool, funny, friendly…)		
6. Who does he / she look like?		
7. What color are his / her eyes?		
8. What color is his / her hair?		
9. What are his / her hobbies? (jogging, reading, cooking…)		
10. What's his / her favorite food?		
11. Who's his / her favorite singer?		
12. What's his / her favorite movie?		

2 Ask more questions about your partner's friend. Complete the sentences.

1. My friend is _____, but my partner's friend is _____.
2. They both have _____.
3. They both are _____.
4. They both like _____.

> My best friend has…. How about yours?

Smart Talk • Student A

Unit 9—*Don't miss it!*
Student A

 1 PAIR WORK. Read about New Year's Eve in New York City. Then ask questions to complete the text.

A How many people go to Times Square on New Year's Eve?
B 500,000.
A What can you...?

New Year's Eve in Times Square

Every year on December 31st (New Year's Eve), _____ people go to Times Square in New York. (How many?) It's a great place to be. You can see firework displays and hear _____. (What?) You can even vote for the music by _____! (How?) You can also see a lot of _____. (Who?)

It's free, but you have to get there _____ (When?) if you want to see anything. And when you're in Times Square, you can't move. You have to stay there until _____ (Who?) goes home!

2 Now read about the Calgary Stampede in Canada. Then answer your partner's questions.

Chuckwagon race at the Calgary Stampede

Each year, millions of visitors from around the world come to Calgary, Alberta for the Calgary Stampede. It's Canada's biggest party! You can see a rodeo, you can listen to music from top Canadian music stars, and, best of all, you can watch chuckwagon races.

Chuckwagons were very common here in the 1800s. Now you can see them in races! Four wagons and 16 cowboys race around a track. It's very exciting—and very dangerous!

Or you can just watch the people. In downtown Calgary, people dress like cowboys, with jeans, cowboy boots, and white hats.

And don't miss the parade! The chuckwagons are there, and they aren't racing, so you can take photographs of them!

Smart Talk • Student A

Unit 10—*Is there a bank?*
Student A

 1 PAIR WORK. Ask and answer questions to complete the map. Ask about the places in the box.

A Is there a <u>bookstore</u>?
B No, there isn't.
A Is there a <u>bank</u>?
B Yes, there is. It's next to the <u>hotel</u>.

Places
bookstore
bank
convenience store
gym
department store
Internet cafe

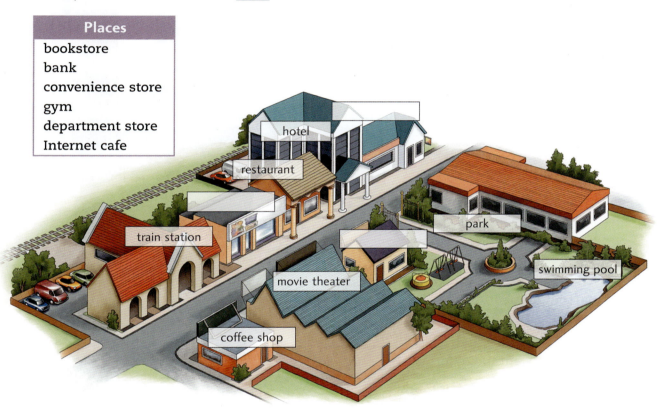

2 Talk about the area near your school. Complete the sentences.

1. There's a convenience store _____.
2. There's a post office _____.
3. There's a _____ around here, but there isn't a _____.
4. There are some good _____ around here.
5. There aren't any good _____ around here.
6. There _____ a department store around here.
7. There are _____ train stations around here.

Is there a…?

Are there any good…?

There's a ___, but is there a ___?

93

Smart Talk • Student A

Unit 11—*What did you do there?*
Student A

 1 PAIR WORK. Look at the pictures from Matt's vacation. Then ask your partner questions to complete the information.

A Did Matt go to <u>the US</u>?
B No, he didn't.
A Did he go to <u>Australia</u>?
B Yes, he did. That's right!

Matt's vacation
1. He went to <u>Australia</u>.
2. He went with his _____.
3. He arrived at _____ o'clock.
4. He visited _____.
5. He saw some _____.
6. He met some people from _____.
7. He had a _____ time.

2 Now look at the information about Amy's vacation. Answer your partner's questions.

Amy's vacation
1. She went to California.
2. She went with her brother.
3. She arrived at three o'clock.
4. She visited Hollywood.
5. She ate Mexican food.
6. She met some people from Brazil.
7. She had a good time.

94

Smart Talk • Student A

Unit 12—*Where are they going to go?*
Student A

 1 PAIR WORK. Ask and answer questions to complete the information. Try to guess the place.

A Where is Fernando going to go on his next trip? <u>Tokyo</u>?
B No, he's going to go to <u>Seoul</u>.

1. Fernando
   Where: <u>Seoul</u>
   How: _____
   When: _____
   How long: _____
   Who with: _____

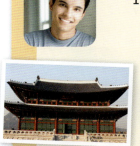

4. Ya-ting
   Where: Monterrey
   How: bicycle
   When: next month
   How long: a weekend
   Who with: best friend

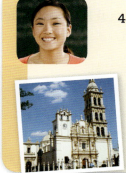

2. Dino
   Where: Dubai
   How: bus
   When: the summer
   How long: a week
   Who with: family

5. Carla
   Where: _____
   How: _____
   When: _____
   How long: _____
   Who with: _____

3. Brian
   Where: _____
   How: _____
   When: _____
   How long: _____
   Who with: _____

6. Amy
   Where: Okinawa
   How: plane
   When: the fall
   How long: a month
   Who with: brother

2 Ask your partner about future plans. Complete the sentences.

1. On Friday night, my partner is going to _____.
2. My partner is going to go by _____.
3. Next week, my partner _____.
4. My partner isn't going to _____ by _____.
5. My partner and I are both _____.

> What are you going to do on...?

> I'm going to.... How about you?

95

Smart Talk

Unit 1—Who's that?
Student B

1 PAIR WORK. Ask and answer questions to complete the information.

A Who's <u>number 1</u>?
B That's <u>Bono</u>. What's <u>his</u> real name?
A <u>His</u> real name is <u>Paul Hewson</u>. Where is <u>he</u> from?
B <u>He's</u> from <u>Ireland</u>.

Useful Language
How do you spell that?
Can you repeat that?
Did you say … ?

1. **Name:** Bono
   Real Name: ____Paul Hewson____
   From: Ireland

2. **Name:** Kaká
   Real Name: _____
   _____
   From: Brazil

3. **Name:** _____
   Real Name: Jennifer Anastassakis
   From: _____

4. **Name:** Shaq
   Real Name: _____
   _____
   From: the US

5. **Name:** _____
   Real Name: Yeoh Choo-Kheng
   From: _____

6. **Name:** Jim Carrey
   Real Name: _____
   _____
   From: Canada

2 Ask about your partner's favorite stars. Complete the sentences.

1. My partner's favorite singer is _____.
2. He / She is from _____.
3. My partner's favorite actor is _____.
4. He / She is from _____.
5. My partner's favorite athlete is _____.
6. His / Her real name is _____.

Who's your favorite…?

Where's she from?

What's his real name?

96

Smart Talk • Student B

Unit 2—*What do they do?*
Student B

1 PAIR WORK. Look at the pictures. Ask and answer questions to complete the information.

A What <u>does Robin</u> do?
B <u>She's a doctor.</u>
A Where <u>does she</u> work?
B <u>She works</u> in <u>a hospital</u>.

1. Robin
   Job: doctor
   Works in: a hospital

2. Alan
   Job: _____
   Works in: _____

3. Jane and Kim
   Job: chefs
   Works in: a restaurant

4. Mark and Yuko
   Job: _____
   Works in: _____

5. Sang
   Job: clerk
   Works in: a convenience store

6. Erika
   Job: _____
   Works in: _____

2 Ask your partner about these people. Write their jobs.

1. My partner is _____.
2. My partner's dad is _____.
3. My partner's mom is _____.
4. My partner's friend is _____.
5. _____ is my partner's dream job.

Useful Words

What does your ___ do?
What's your dream job?

a businessman / businesswoman
a housewife   an office worker
an assistant   between jobs
self-employed

97

Smart Talk • Student B

Unit 3—*Does he like fish?*
Student B

1 PAIR WORK. Ask and answer questions to complete the chart. Ask about the six food items.

A Does Joe <u>love</u> <u>ice cream</u>?
B No, he doesn't.
A Does he <u>love</u> <u>salad</u>?
B No, he doesn't.
A Does he <u>love</u> <u>fish</u>?
B Yes, he does. That's right!

Food

2 Ask and answer questions to complete the sentences.

1. I like _____, but my partner doesn't.
2. I don't like _____, but my partner does.
3. My partner and I both like _____ and _____.
4. We both don't like _____ and _____.
5. We both love _____.

Do you like ___?

I don't like ___. How about you?

I don't like ___ either.

Smart Talk • Student B

Unit 4—*How often?*
Student B

 1 PAIR WORK. Ask and answer questions to complete the chart.

A What does <u>Amy</u> do to keep fit?
B She <u>goes swimming</u>.
A How often does she <u>go swimming</u>?
B <u>Twice a week</u>.
A Does she like it?
B <u>Yes, she does.</u> It's fun!

	What do they do to keep fit?	How often?	Do they like it?
Amy	swimming	twice a week	Yes. It's fun!
Chris			
Sara	tennis	every weekend	Yes. But it's expensive.
Gabriel			
Kim and Max	bicycling	every morning	Yes. They go fast!

2 What does your partner do to keep fit? Complete the sentences.

1. My partner _____ goes to the gym.
2. My partner _____ plays basketball.
3. My partner _____ does yoga.
4. My partner _____ goes swimming.
5. My partner _____ goes bicycling.

Smart Talk • Student B

Unit 5—What is he doing?
Student B

1 PAIR WORK. Look at the people. Who are they? Ask and answer questions with a partner. Ask about the names in the box.

A Is <u>Ellen</u> <u>talking on the phone</u>?
B No, she's not.
A Is she <u>checking her e-mail</u>?
B Yes, she is.

Names
Dan
Paul
Henry
Mike
Bill

2 What is your partner doing right now? Check (✓) *True* or *False*.

	True	False
1. My partner is sending a text message.	☐	☐
2. My partner is thinking about lunch.	☐	☐
3. My partner is looking at the teacher.	☐	☐
4. My partner is daydreaming.	☐	☐
5. My partner is speaking in English.	☐	☐

Are you ___ right now?

Yes, I am. How about you?

Smart Talk • Student B

Unit 6—*Where were they?*
Student B

1 PAIR WORK. Look at the people. Where were they on Saturday? Where are they now? Ask and answer questions to complete the information.

   A Where <u>was Tom</u> on Saturday?
   B <u>He was at a party</u>. Where <u>is he</u> now?
   A <u>He's in class</u>.

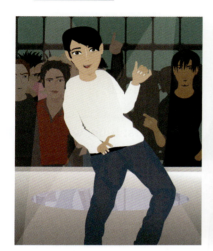

1. Tom
   Saturday: at a party
   Now: ____in class____

2. Miho
   Saturday: on a plane
   Now: _____

3. Amy and Jen
   Saturday: _____
   Now: in the hospital

4. Susan
   Saturday: at the gym
   Now: _____

5. Bill and Mary
   Saturday: _____
   Now: at a concert

6. Mike
   Saturday: at the beach
   Now: _____

2 Ask your partner about the people. Where were they on Saturday?

   1. My partner was _____ on Saturday.
   2. My partner's friend was _____ on Saturday.
   3. My partner's brother / sister was _____ on Saturday.
   4. My partner's parents were _____ on Saturday.

Where were you…?

Where was your…?

101

Smart Talk • Student B

Unit 7—Which one do you like?
Student B

 1 PAIR WORK. Look at the pictures. Ask and answer questions to complete the information.

A How much <u>are the jeans</u>?
B <u>They're $35</u>. Where are <u>they</u> from?
A <u>They're</u> from <u>the US</u>. What <u>colors</u> do you have?
B <u>Blue, black, or green.</u>

1. Jeans
   Price: $35
   From: ___the US___
   Colors: Blue, black, green

2. Baggy pants
   Price: $60
   From: _____
   Colors: Blue, white, black

3. Sweater
   Price: _____
   From: Scotland
   Sizes: _____

4. Sweatshirt
   Price: $30
   From: _____
   Sizes: Small, medium, large

5. T-shirt
   Price: _____
   From: France
   Styles: _____

6. Shirt
   Price: $100
   From: _____
   Styles: Long-sleeved only

7. High heels
   Price: _____
   From: Italy
   Colors: _____

8. Sneakers
   Price: $75
   From: _____
   Colors: White, red, black

2 Compare the clothes in each row. Which do you like? Why?

A Which do you like, the <u>jeans</u> or the <u>baggy pants</u>?
B I like <u>the baggy pants</u>.
A Really? Why?
B I think they're <u>more comfortable</u>. How about you?
A I like <u>the jeans</u>. They're <u>more practical</u>.
  And <u>they're cheaper</u>!

Useful Words

cheap	fashionable
colorful	nice
comfortable	practical
elegant	stylish
expensive	warm

102

Smart Talk • Student B

Unit 8—*My best friend*
Student B

1 PAIR WORK. Answer the questions about your best friend. Then compare answers with a partner. Write your partner's answers in the survey.

A What's his or her name?
B It's <u>Maria</u>.
A Where is she from?
B <u>She's</u> from <u>Mexico City</u>.
A When is <u>her</u> birthday?
B <u>I'm not sure</u>.

	My best friend	My partner's best friend
1. What's his / her name?		
2. Where is he / she from?		
3. How old is he / she?		
4. When is his / her birthday?		
5. What's he / she like? (smart, cool, funny, friendly…)		
6. Who does he / she look like?		
7. What color are his / her eyes?		
8. What color is his / her hair?		
9. What are his / her hobbies? (jogging, reading, cooking…)		
10. What's his / her favorite food?		
11. Who's his / her favorite singer?		
12. What's his / her favorite movie?		

2 Ask more questions about your partner's friend. Complete the sentences.

1. My friend is _____, but my partner's friend is _____.
2. They both have _____.
3. They both are _____.
4. They both like _____.

> My best friend has....
> How about yours?

103

Smart Talk • Student B

Unit 9—Don't miss it!
Student B

 1 PAIR WORK. Read about New Year's Eve in New York City. Then answer your partner's questions.

A How many people go to Times Square on New Year's Eve?
B 500,000.
A What can you...?

New Year's Eve in Times Square

Every year on December 31st (New Year's Eve), 500,000 people go to Times Square in New York. It's a great place to be. You can see firework displays and hear great music. You can even vote for the music by sending a text message! You can also see a lot of famous people.

It's free, but you have to get there early if you want to see anything. And when you're in Times Square, you can't move. You have to stay there until everyone goes home!

2 Now read about the Calgary Stampede in Canada. Then ask questions to complete the text.

Chuckwagon race at the Calgary Stampede

Each year, millions of visitors from around the world come to Calgary, Alberta for the Calgary Stampede. It's Canada's biggest party! You can see a rodeo, you can listen to _____, (What?) and, best of all, you can watch _____. (What?)

Chuckwagons were very common here in the 1800s. Now you can see them _____! (Where?) Four wagons and 16 cowboys race around a track. It's very exciting—and very dangerous!

Or you can just watch _____. (Who?) In downtown Calgary, people dress like cowboys, with jeans, cowboy boots, and white hats.

And don't miss the parade! The _____ are there, (What?) and they aren't racing, so you can take photographs of them!

104

Smart Talk • Student B

Unit 10 — *Is there a bank?*
Student B

 1 PAIR WORK. Ask and answer questions to complete the map. Ask about the places in the box.

- A Is there a <u>bookstore</u>?
- B No, there isn't.
- A Is there a <u>bank</u>?
- B Yes, there is. It's next to the <u>hotel</u>.

Places
restaurant
post office
shopping mall
swimming pool
shoe store
movie theater

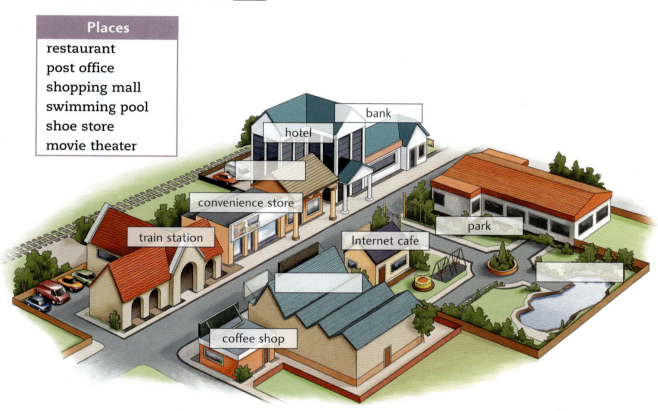

2 Talk about the area near your school. Complete the sentences.

1. There's a convenience store _____.
2. There's a post office _____.
3. There's a _____ around here, but there isn't a _____.
4. There are some good _____ around here.
5. There aren't any good _____ around here.
6. There _____ a department store around here.
7. There are _____ train stations around here.

Is there a…?

Are there any good…?

There's a ___, but is there a ___?

105

Smart Talk • Student B

Unit 11—What did you do there?
Student B

1 PAIR WORK. Look at the information about Matt's vacation. Then answer your partner's questions.

A Did Matt go to <u>the US</u>?
B No, he didn't.
A Did he go to <u>Australia</u>?
B Yes, he did. That's right!

Matt's vacation
1. He went to Australia.
2. He went with his friend.
3. He arrived at twelve o'clock.
4. He visited Sydney.
5. He saw some kangaroos.
6. He met some people from Canada.
7. He had a great time.

2 Now look at the pictures from Amy's vacation. Ask your partner questions to complete the information.

Amy's vacation
1. She went to _____.
2. She went with her _____.
3. She arrived at _____ o'clock.
4. She visited _____.
5. She ate _____ food.
6. She met some people from _____.
7. She had a _____ time.

Smart Talk • Student B

Unit 12—Where are they going to go?
Student B

 1 PAIR WORK. Ask and answer questions to complete the information. Try to guess the place.

A Where is Fernando going to go on his next trip? <u>Tokyo</u>?
B No, he's going to go to <u>Seoul</u>.

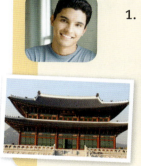

1. Fernando
   Where: Seoul
   How: car
   When: next week
   How long: two weeks
   Who with: sister

4. Ya-ting
   Where: _____
   How: _____
   When: _____
   How long: _____
   Who with: _____

2. Dino
   Where: _____
   How: _____
   When: _____
   How long: _____
   Who with: _____

5. Carla
   Where: Hanoi
   How: train
   When: next year
   How long: three months
   Who with: friend

3. Brian
   Where: Salvador
   How: plane
   When: the spring
   How long: five days
   Who with: parents

6. Amy
   Where: _____
   How: _____
   When: _____
   How long: _____
   Who with: _____

2 Ask your partner about future plans. Complete the sentences.

1. On Friday night, my partner is going to _____.
2. My partner is going to go by _____.
3. Next week, my partner _____.
4. My partner isn't going to _____ by _____.
5. My partner and I are both _____.

> What are you going to do on...?

> I'm going to.... How about you?

Unit 1

1 Read this information from a pen pal. Then write a similar e-mail about yourself.

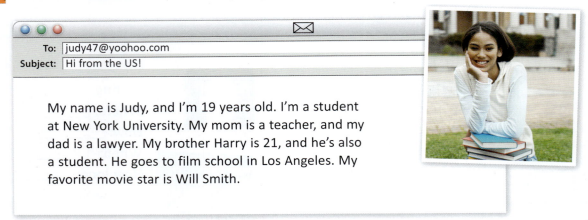

2 PAIR WORK. Take turns reading your e-mails. Ask your partner questions about his or her e-mail.

Unit 2

1 Complete the form with your personal information. Then use the information to write a paragraph about yourself.

Hi! My name is Sang-hyuk Lee. I'm Korean, from Seoul, but I live in Japan. I work for a car company in Tokyo.

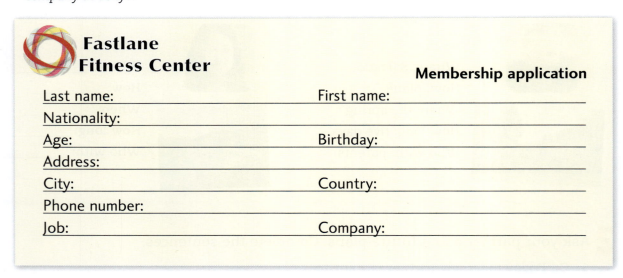

2 PAIR WORK. Compare paragraphs with your partner. What else do you want to know? Ask questions.

108

Unit 3

1 Read the letter from a teenager in the US. Then write a similar letter about your favorite restaurant.

> Hey! How's everything?
>
> This is a photo of me and my friend Julie. We're at our favorite Japanese restaurant. We *love* Japanese food! Do you like Japanese food? My favorite Japanese food is sushi. What about you?
>
> Talk to you soon!
>
> Megan

2 GROUP WORK. Compare letters with your group. Which restaurant does your group like best?

Unit 4

1 Read the e-mail from a pen pal. Then write a reply. What do you usually do on…

- Saturday morning?
- Saturday afternoon?
- Saturday night?
- Sunday morning, afternoon, and night?

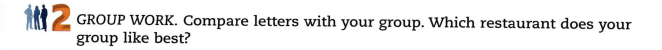

To: lee01@inter.com
Subject: Hi! It's Friday!

Hi! It's Friday! The weekend! I'm so happy. I love weekends. I usually stay in bed all morning on Saturday. Then in the afternoon, I go to the mall and meet my friends. At night, we usually go to a party. On Sunday, I sleep all morning—again!—and in the afternoon, I watch soccer on TV. At night, I do some homework.

What about you? What do you do on the weekend?

2 PAIR WORK. Take turns reading your e-mails. Make a list of things you both usually do on the weekend.

Writing

Unit 5

1 Complete the online conversation. Read the questions before and after the answers you write. Then write a paragraph about what you are doing right now.

Right now I'm doing my homework at my friend's house...

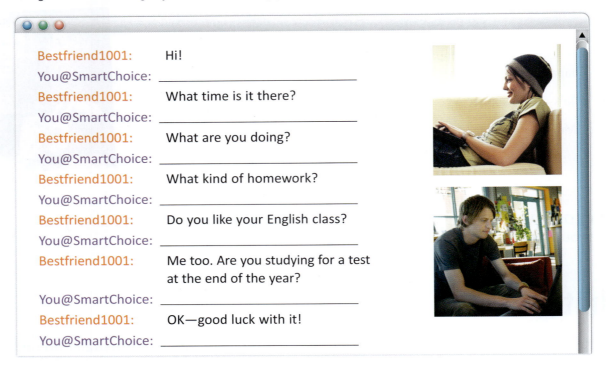

Bestfriend1001:	Hi!
You@SmartChoice:	_____
Bestfriend1001:	What time is it there?
You@SmartChoice:	_____
Bestfriend1001:	What are you doing?
You@SmartChoice:	_____
Bestfriend1001:	What kind of homework?
You@SmartChoice:	_____
Bestfriend1001:	Do you like your English class?
You@SmartChoice:	_____
Bestfriend1001:	Me too. Are you studying for a test at the end of the year?
You@SmartChoice:	_____
Bestfriend1001:	OK—good luck with it!
You@SmartChoice:	_____

2 PAIR WORK. Compare paragraphs with a partner. Find two differences between you and your partner.

Unit 6

1 Read Marco's diary about his last English class. Then write similar information about your last English class.

> My last English class was on Tuesday. The weather was cold, and the sky was gray. My bus was late so I was late for class. The class was at 4:00 p.m. Mr. Dawson was the teacher. He was on time. Eighteen students were there. It was a really fun class. But now I have too much homework!

2 PAIR WORK. Compare your writing with a partner. Did you both like your last class?

110

Writing

Unit 7

1 Read this e-mail from a pen pal. Then write a reply. Be sure to answer these questions:

- Are you interested in clothes?
- What kind of clothes do you like?
- What do you wear at school (or work)?
- Are there any rules about what you can wear there?

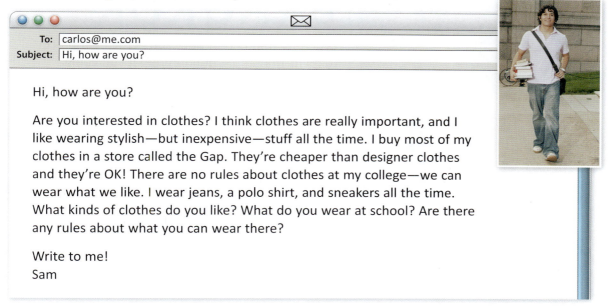

To: carlos@me.com
Subject: Hi, how are you?

Hi, how are you?

Are you interested in clothes? I think clothes are really important, and I like wearing stylish—but inexpensive—stuff all the time. I buy most of my clothes in a store called the Gap. They're cheaper than designer clothes and they're OK! There are no rules about clothes at my college—we can wear what we like. I wear jeans, a polo shirt, and sneakers all the time. What kinds of clothes do you like? What do you wear at school? Are there any rules about what you can wear there?

Write to me!
Sam

2 PAIR WORK. Take turns reading your e-mails. Do you and your partner like the same clothes? Find two differences.

Unit 8

1 Read the information about Tony. Then write a similar paragraph about yourself. What are you like? What do you look like?

Pen Pals International

Please write a paragraph about yourself for our files. Include what you look like, your personality, what your friends think of you, and who you want to write to.

My name is Tony. I'm from Los Angeles, and I'm a medical student. I'm tall and athletic-looking. I work hard in med school, but I also enjoy my free time. I play a lot of soccer, I ski, and I windsurf. I'm friendly, and I'm pretty funny. My friends like me—I think! I want to write to people in Asia—Korea, Vietnam, places like that.

2 PAIR WORK. Compare paragraphs with a partner. Ask your partner questions.

111

Writing

Unit 9

1 Read this article about places in Thailand. Then write a similar article about your town or country. Recommend something different for visitors to do.

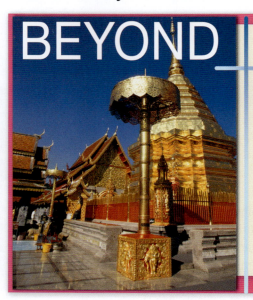

BEYOND BANGKOK

Everyone thinks that Bangkok is the best place to go in Thailand. I don't agree! If you come to Thailand, you should visit other places. My favorite place in Thailand is Chiang Mai. It's a smaller city, it has great food, and some really interesting people live there—like me! You can get there by train from Bangkok. It takes six or seven hours.

2 PAIR WORK. Take turns reading your articles. What else can you recommend for visitors to do in your town?

Unit 10

1 Read this e-mail from a US student living in Mexico City. Then write a similar paragraph about the street where you live.

> Right now, I'm living in a student hostel in an area called the Zona Rosa. It's very busy! There are some huge stores at the other end of my street. Fortunately, my part of the street is quieter. There are only a few small stores, and there aren't many people. But there's always a lot of traffic, day and night, so it's very noisy.
>
> In my hometown in the US, I live on a very quiet street. There aren't any stores, just houses. And every house has a front yard and a backyard.

2 PAIR WORK. Compare paragraphs with a partner. Are your streets similar or very different?

Writing

Unit 11

1 Read about Jack's best and worst vacations. Then write a similar paragraph about your best (or worst!) vacation.

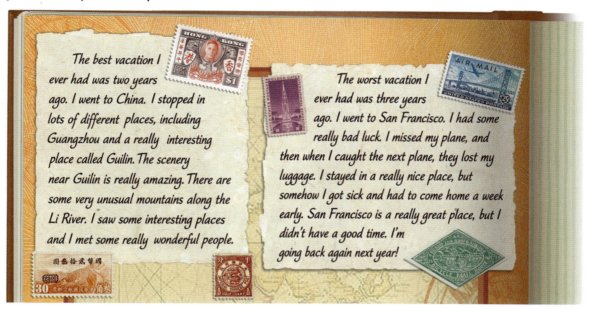

The best vacation I ever had was two years ago. I went to China. I stopped in lots of different places, including Guangzhou and a really interesting place called Guilin. The scenery near Guilin is really amazing. There are some very unusual mountains along the Li River. I saw some interesting places and I met some really wonderful people.

The worst vacation I ever had was three years ago. I went to San Francisco. I had some really bad luck. I missed my plane, and then when I caught the next plane, they lost my luggage. I stayed in a really nice place, but somehow I got sick and had to come home a week early. San Francisco is a really great place, but I didn't have a good time. I'm going back again next year!

2 GROUP WORK. Take turns reading your paragraphs. Which person's vacation was the best? Which was the worst?

Unit 12

1 Read this e-mail from a Canadian student who wants to study in your country. Then write a reply. Include this information:

- your name
- the name of your city
- the transportation in your city
- things to do in your city

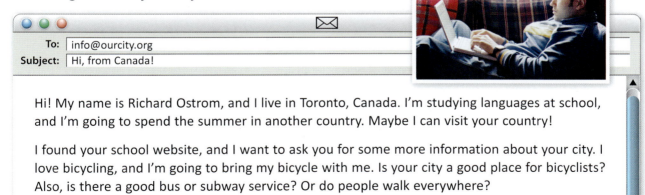

To: info@ourcity.org
Subject: Hi, from Canada!

Hi! My name is Richard Ostrom, and I live in Toronto, Canada. I'm studying languages at school, and I'm going to spend the summer in another country. Maybe I can visit your country!

I found your school website, and I want to ask you for some more information about your city. I love bicycling, and I'm going to bring my bicycle with me. Is your city a good place for bicyclists? Also, is there a good bus or subway service? Or do people walk everywhere?

I hope to hear from you soon!

2 GROUP WORK. Compare your e-mails. What did you say about your city?

113

Audio Scripts

Unit 1

Listening . . . . p. 8

Activity 1

1. What's her name?
2. He's from the US.
3. Where's he from?
4. How are you?
5. They're from Canada.
6. Is she a teacher?

Activity 2

1. Hi, how are you?
2. What's your name?
3. Nice to meet you.
4. Who's that girl over there?
5. Where's she from?
6. Is she your girlfriend?

Unit 2

Listening . . . . p. 13

1. **A** Hi, Jane!
   B Hi... um, sorry, do I know you?
   A Yes! My name is Bob Hamilton. We went to high school together.
   B Oh, Bob, yes. How are you?
   A Fine. Do you still live here in Boston?
   B No, no... I don't live here anymore. I'm on vacation.
   A Where do you live?
   B In New York.
   A And what do you do?
   B I'm a model.
   A A model! How cool is that? Where do you work?
   B Well, I work in a lot of places, but mainly in New York.

2. **A** Ladies and gentlemen, please welcome one of our favorite actors—Joe Dawson! Welcome to the show, Joe.
   B Thanks very much. It's great to be back in Hollywood.
   A Right. You don't live here now, do you?
   B That's right. I'm from Hollywood, but I don't live here now.
   A Where do you live?
   B I live in Miami.
   A Miami? You work in Hollywood, and you live in Miami? Come on!

B Well, actually, my wife is from Miami. Her mom and dad live there.
A Is that right?
B Yes.

3. **A** OK, here's my application!
   B Thank you. So, your name is Alice, and you're from Canada.
   A That's right.
   B Where do you live in Canada?
   A Well, I'm from Toronto, but I live in Vancouver.
   B And what do you do?
   A I'm a student.

Listening Plus . . . . p. 13

A So you're a model.
B Yes. And I'm also a singer.
A Really? That's very cool.
B Um… what do you do, Bob?
A Me? I'm a pilot.
B A pilot?
A Yes.
B Do you work for an airline?
A No, I don't work for an airline.
B Who do you work for?
A Well, I work for a very rich man.
B Oh, yeah?
A Yes, he's a famous Hollywood producer.
B He's a what?
A A Hollywood producer?
B Really?
A Yes. Well, nice to see you again, Jane.
B Yes! Nice to see you, too, Bob.
A Bye.
B Hey… wait!

Unit 3

Listening . . . . p. 19

1. **A** Hi! Welcome to New Asia Restaurant. How are you tonight?
   B Good, thanks. Can I see a menu, please?
   A Sure. Here you are.
   B Wow. You have so many foods. What's your favorite?
   A Well, the noodles are really good, but I like the beef and rice.
   B OK. I'll have the beef and rice.
   A One order of beef and rice, coming right up!

114

2. A Welcome to Cafe Roma. How are you?
  B I'm pretty good, thanks. Do you have a menu?
  A Yes, we do. Here it is.
  B Hey, what a big menu! Lasagna, pizza… You have everything!
  A We sure do. Anything Italian, anyway.
  B Well, I like pasta. Mmm, spaghetti. I'll have that.
  A One spaghetti. Good choice, sir.

3. A Hi, welcome to Donna's Diner.
  B Thank you. Um, is there a menu?
  A Yeah, it's right there on the table.
  B Oh, right. Hmm. Hamburger, cheeseburger, club sandwich…
  A The cheeseburgers are really good here.
  B Really? I like cheeseburgers. Actually, I *love* cheeseburgers, but I'm on a diet. I'll just have a salad.
  A Sir, are you sure?
  B Yeah, I'm sure.

Listening Plus . . . . p. 19

1. A Do you like your beef and rice?
  B Actually, no. It's very salty.
  A Oh, no. I'm sorry. Do you want some water?
  B Oh, please. That'd be great.

2. A How is everything?
  B It's very good, thank you.
  A Do you like your spaghetti?
  B Yes, it's great.
  A Can I get you anything else?
  B Um, yes, actually. I'm really hungry today! I'll have a cheese sandwich.
  A OK, I'll bring a cheese sandwich.

3. A Do you like your salad?
  B Yes, I do. It's delicious! But I'm still hungry.
  A Can I get you something else?
  B Well, I don't know. I'm on a diet.
  A How about some soup?
  B Um, no…
  A A soda?
  B No, thanks. Oh, I'll have a cheeseburger. I'll start my diet tomorrow.

Unit 4

Listening . . . . p. 27

1. A Hello everyone, and welcome to the show. I'm downtown today to ask people: How do *you* keep fit? Let's find out. Excuse me? Can I interview you?
  B Yeah, sure.

  A Great. First, what's your name, and how old are you?
  B My name's Greg, and I'm 20. I'm a college student.
  A And what do you do to keep fit?
  B I go swimming at the beach.
  A And how often do you go swimming?
  B Every morning.
  A Wow. OK, thanks!

2. A Excuse me! Hi, there. Can I interview you?
  B Sure. What do you want to know?
  A Well, first, what's your name, and how old are you?
  B I'm Alice, and I'm 27.
  A OK. So what do you do to keep fit?
  B Well, I'm a student. I study art. So I don't have time to exercise. But I sometimes visit museums. That's a lot of walking, you know.
  A Right. So how often do you visit museums?
  B Oh, probably two days a week.
  A Sounds good. Thanks!

3. A Oh, sir? Sir? Can I interview you?
  B Why not?
  A OK. What's your name, and how old are you?
  B My name is Tom, and I'm 39.
  A How old?
  B 39.
  A OK. And how do you keep fit?
  B Well, I don't really exercise. Sometimes I go bowling, but that's all.
  A Well, that's exercise. How often do you go bowling?
  B Once a week. On Wednesdays.
  A Thanks.

Listening Plus . . . . p. 27

1. A Greg, can I ask you another question?
  B Sure.
  A You go swimming at the beach every morning, right?
  B Right.
  A In the summer and winter?
  B No way! Not in the winter! I never go swimming at the beach in the winter. It's too cold.
  A So what do you do to keep fit in the winter?
  B Well, I walk a lot, and I sometimes go jogging.
  A How often?
  B Um… maybe three times a week?
  A Thank you.

2. A Uh, hello again, Alice.
  B Yes?
  A Can I ask you another question?
  B Sure. Go ahead.

Audio Scripts

A You walk to keep fit, right?
B Yes.
A Do you go the gym at all?
B No, never.
A Never?
B Right.
A Why not?
B I don't like the gym, because it's always crowded. And really, I don't have time!
A Thank you.

3. **A** Excuse me, Tom?
B Yes?
A Can I ask another question?
B Sure.
A Do you go the gym?
B Me? The gym? No way.
A Why not?
B Because I'm 39.
A And…?
B And the people in the gym are all too young!
A Oh, OK. Thank you.

Unit 5

Listening . . . . p. 33

1. **A** Hello?
B Hi, Joe, this is Diane.
A Oh, hi. How are things?
B Good. Joe, I'm looking at your last math exercise on the computer.
A Uh-huh?
B It's not bad, but… Joe, what are you doing?
A I'm watching TV.
B I see. What are you watching?
A A football game.
B What about your math homework?
A I'm doing that, too.
B You're doing your math homework, and you're watching a football game on TV?
A Yes.
B Joe, you can't do both! Turn off the TV, and do your homework!

2. **A** Hello, this is Susie.
B Hi, Susie! This is Maria. How's it going?
A Oh, hi, Maria. I'm just at the coffee shop. I'm reading a book about Japan.
B Is it interesting?
A Yeah, it really is. What are you doing?
B I'm reading.

A What are you reading?
B An exercise magazine.
A Is that interesting?
B Well, no, not really.

3. **A** Hello, Richard Smith speaking.
B Hi, Richard. This is Don. What are you doing?
A I'm talking to you!
B Very funny. I mean, like, are you studying?
A I sure am. I'm doing my computer science homework.
B Really? Is it interesting?
A Not really. But it's important. What are you doing?
B I'm cooking spaghetti!
A Mmm! Can I come over and have some?

Listening Plus . . . . p. 33

A Joe, please stop watching TV and do some work.
B Diane, it's a really good game.
A Joe, your mother pays me to be your math tutor. Turn off the TV!
B OK, OK…
A Are you turning it off?
B Yes, I am.
A Good. Do you have your math book there?
B Yes, I do.
A OK. Please open it.
B OK.
A Is your book open?
B Yes.
A Joe, listen to me. This is important. You're good at math, but you don't work hard.
B I know, I know. The book is open. I'm looking at it now.
A What page are you looking at?
B Huh?
A Which page are you looking at?
B Uh, page 18?
A OK. Tell me the first exercise.
B Um, hold on a second.
A Joe, are you watching TV again?

Unit 6

Listening . . . . p. 39

1. **A** Good afternoon, sir. Ticket, please.
B I'm sorry I'm late. The traffic was terrible.
A Yes, I know. Now, may I see your ticket?
B And my plane leaves in five minutes!
A It's all right, sir. Just give me your ticket.

116

Audio Scripts

B No problem. It's here… I think… I've got it… somewhere. Oh, boy! It was in my pocket this morning!

A Is it in your pocket now?

B No, it isn't.

A How about your suitcase?

B Oh, my suitcase! No, it isn't.

A How about your bag?

B My bag? No, it isn't.

2. A Hi! I'm so sorry I'm late. I was really busy at work.

B Don't worry. It's no problem.

A And my boss was really impossible!

B It's OK. You're here now. Do you have the tickets?

A What? The tickets? No, you have them.

B No, I don't. They were on the kitchen table.

A They were?

B Yes, they were.

A I see. I guess they're still on the kitchen table.

B Right.

3. A Hi, guys!

B/C Hi!

A Sorry I'm late. I was on the phone with my mom.

B That's OK. So are you ready? Let's go to the beach!

A The beach? But I was at the beach yesterday.

B You were?

A Yeah. Aren't we going to the mountains today?

B/C Oh! We were at the mountains yesterday!

A So, no beach, no mountains. Where are we going?

B I don't know. How about the mall?

A Well, all right.

Listening Plus . . . . p. 39

A This is crazy! My ticket isn't in my pocket, and it isn't in my bag. And oh, no! Where's my passport? I don't have my passport!

B It's OK, sir. Calm down.

A Calm down? My ticket and my passport were in my pocket this morning. I'm sure they were!

B OK, sir. So where were you this morning? Were you at home?

A At home? No, I wasn't at home! I was in a hotel.

B Which hotel?

A What?

B Which hotel were you in?

A The Excelsior. And my ticket… Oh, no…

B What is it?

A My ticket and passport were on the table in my room.

B Oh, OK…

A I was late, you see. I was in a hurry.

B Yes, sir. Don't worry. Oh, what's that?

A What?

B On the floor. I think it's your ticket and your passport.

A Oh! Thank you! You're a star!

B You're welcome.

Unit 7

Listening . . . . p. 47

1. A Hi, can I help you?

B Yeah, I'm looking for some jeans.

A Great. We have a lot of jeans. How about these designer jeans?

B I don't know. Aren't designer jeans expensive?

A Well, these are $160. Is that expensive?

B Yeah, it is. Do you have anything else?

A Oh, these regular jeans are $49.99, but the designer jeans are cooler.

B Yeah, but the regular jeans aren't as expensive! I'll take the regular jeans.

2. A Hi! How can I help you?

B I need a new pair of high heels.

A OK. What about these? They're from Italy.

B They're very nice. How much are they?

A A hundred and ninety dollars.

B Oh, no. I need something cheaper.

A OK, how about these? They're $65.

B They're perfect. I'll buy them.

3. A Good morning. How can I help you?

B I want to buy a jacket.

A Sure. Try this blue one. It's only $30.

B Let me try it on. I don't know. Do you have anything more comfortable?

A Well, there's this brown jacket. It's made in Italy. It's very comfortable…

B Yeah!

A …but very expensive. It's $200.

B Oh, that's no problem. I want it!

A Are you sure? The blue one is cheaper.

B It's OK. I have my mom's credit card. Give me the Italian jacket!

4. A Hi! Need any help?

B Yeah. I need a new sweater.

A This red one is good. It's only $39.99.

B Yeah, but I want a more colorful one.

A Well, this one is more colorful, but it's $170.

B Oh, that's a lot. The red one is cheaper.

A It's a difficult decision.

B Yeah. Hmm. All right, why not? Give me the expensive sweater. I work hard. I deserve it!

117

Audio Scripts

Listening Plus . . . . p. 47

1. A So, you want the regular jeans.
B Yes.
A Are you sure?
B Yes. Why? What's the problem?
A Nothing! But they aren't as nice as the designer jeans.
B I know that, but the designer jeans are so expensive!
A Well, that's right, but everyone is wearing them this year.
B Really?
A Yes. We sell more designer jeans than regular jeans. No one is buying cheaper jeans.
B No one is buying the cheaper jeans?
A No.
B Are you sure about that?
A Oh, yes!
B Good. I want the cheaper jeans.
A You do?
B Yes.
A Why?
B Who wants to wear the same thing as everyone else?

2. A Are you sure you don't want the Italian shoes?
B Positive.
A OK.
B Why?
A I think the Italian shoes look better on you.
B Me, too, but they're $190.
A But they look better! Think about it. People look at you and say, "Nice dress, but cheap shoes."
B You think so?
A Oh, yes! But if that's what you want, no problem!
B Wait a second. OK… I'll have the more expensive ones.

Unit 8

Listening . . . . p. 53

1. A Hi, I'm Sandy.
B Hello. I'm Elaine.
A Nice party, right?
B Yes.
A So, how do you know my brother?
B Your brother?
A This is my brother Alex's party.

B Oh, right! My boyfriend and Alex were friends in college.
A Is your boyfriend here?
B Yes. He's over there. Near the door.
A Wow! You mean the tall guy with blonde hair? He looks like Brad Pitt!
B Uh, no. The one next to him.
A Oh… the guy with glasses and a mustache?
B Yes.
A Nice!
B Actually, he is. Very nice. Do you want to meet him?
A Sure!

2. A Excuse me, was a young girl here a minute ago?
B Pardon me?
A I'm looking for my daughter. I think she was just here.
B What does she look like?
A She's ten years old. She has curly red hair. Her name is Jane, and she's a very good girl. Very nice and friendly.
B Oh, yes, I think she was here a few minutes ago.
A Where is she now?
B I don't know.

3. A Hello?
B Hi, I'm calling about your ad. Are you looking for a roommate?
A I sure am. Can you tell me about yourself? What are you like?
B Well, I'm 22, and I'm a student.
A Uh-huh, and are you a neat person?
B Neat?
A Yeah, neat. You know, clean. Not messy.
B No, I'm not. Not really.
A Well, uh, sorry, the room isn't free.

4. A Hey, Tom, I saw Ichiro at the mall.
B Really? At the mall? Wow, why was Ichiro there?
A He works there, at the music store.
B What? A baseball star works *there*?
A Baseball star? What are you talking about?
B I'm talking about Ichiro! Ichiro Suzuki, the famous baseball player.
A No, Tom! I mean Ichiro *Ono*. You know, Ichiro from English class!
B Oh.
A Well, he says "hi" to you, anyway.

118

Audio Scripts

Listening Plus . . . . p. 53

A Sandy, this is my boyfriend, John. John, this is Sandy.

B Hi, Sandy, nice to meet you.

C Nice to meet you too, John. So, you were at college with my brother.

B I was?

A Sandy is Alex's sister.

B Oh! You're Alex's sister!

C Yes.

B Are you the famous sister? The TV presenter?

C No, that's my sister Tina.

B Oh, OK. So you're the smart one. You teach at a college, right?

C No. That's my sister Amanda.

B Oh, I'm sorry. So what do you do, Sandy?

C I teach elementary school.

B OK, so you *are* smart.

C Yes, but not as smart as Amanda.

A And not as famous as Tina.

C Right.

Unit 9

Listening . . . . p. 59

1. Hi, my name is Tomas, and I'm from Brazil. I live in Rio de Janeiro—a great place for a vacation! There are so many things you can do. Of course, you can go to the beach, but I want to tell you about Brazilian music. Brazilian people love music, and they love to dance. And in Rio, you can hear some great music. You can hear samba, bossa nova, choro, and even reggae. So this is my advice to you—when you come to Rio, check out the music scene.

2. My name is Gary, and I live in New York City—a great city and a great place to visit! A lot of people visit New York, but they all go to the same places. Everyone goes to the Statue of Liberty, the Empire State Building, Ground Zero… They're all great places, but the best place in New York is the Village, Greenwich Village. You can eat great food, go shopping, or just relax. So here's my advice— sure, see the Statue of Liberty, but after that, chill in Greenwich Village.

3. Hello, my name is Henri, and I live in the beautiful city of Paris. More than a million visitors come to Paris every summer. It's a great city to walk in. There are a lot of interesting places to see. You can see Notre Dame, one of the finest cathedrals in the world. But the best thing to do? This is what I recommend—spend time on our wonderful river, the Seine. You can take a boat tour and see the most famous sights of Paris, in the day or night!

Listening Plus . . . . p. 59

1. After Rio, what do I recommend? Oh, so many places! Let me think… OK, how about Fortaleza? It's on the coast in the northeast of the country. It's an incredible place for a vacation. The nightlife is great, and the beaches are excellent. You can swim every day of the year, and the people there are so relaxed. Food? Do you like fish? The fish in Fortaleza is fabulous. So I recommend Rio first, then Fortaleza.

2. Where can you go after New York City? Well, New Orleans is a really great place. Most people go there for the music and festivals, like Mardi Gras. You can visit some amazing jazz clubs in the French Quarter, and the nightlife there is fantastic, too. The city also has really interesting food—it's a mix of French, Portuguese, Spanish, and Caribbean cooking. It's so delicious! And, of course, the people there are very friendly and nice. They really enjoy life.

3. After Paris? Well, there are some wonderful cities in France—Lyon, Bordeaux, Avignon… but my favorite is Marseilles. Marseilles is a big port in the south of France, on the coast of the Mediterranean Sea. The people in Marseilles are wonderful, very friendly, and very different from the rest of the country. And the food! The food in Marseilles is superb. You can try food from many different cultures there. The port area is good to visit, but be careful if you go there at night. I don't recommend swimming in Marseilles. The beaches are nice, but the water isn't so good.

Unit 10

Listening . . . . p. 67

1. A Hello! How can I help you?

B Yes, is there a swimming pool near here?

A There sure is. It's about two blocks away.

B Oh, good! And when is it open?

A I think it's open from 9 a.m. to 10 p.m.

B Thank you.

A You're welcome. Have a good day!

2. A Hi there! Can I help you?

B Yes, my husband and I are visiting the city for the first time.

A Good! I hope you're enjoying yourself.

119

Audio Scripts

B Oh, we are. But we'd like to go for a walk. Is there a park near here?

A Sure. There's a nice little park on the next block.

B Oh, good. Is it safe there?

A Of course!

B Oh, that's a relief. Thank you so much!

A No problem. Bye!

3. **A** Good morning. How can I help you?

B Well, I want to buy some shoes.

A You're looking for a shoe store?

B Yes, I want to go to a street with a lot of shoe stores.

A No problem. There are a lot of shoe stores on Market Street.

B Market Street. Thanks! Oh, is that far from here?

A Yeah, but you can take a taxi.

B Great. Thanks again!

A You're welcome. Have a nice day.

4. **A** Good afternoon. Can I help you?

B Hi. Wow, this is a great city. You can walk all day. I'm really tired.

A I know.

B I really need some coffee. Is there a coffee shop near here?

A Oh, yes. There's a great place around the corner. It's called Cafe Centro.

B Is it expensive?

A No, not at all.

B Perfect. Thanks so much!

A Don't mention it.

Listening Plus . . . . p. 67

1. **A** Hi! How was the pool?

B Uh, not great. It was too small.

A Oh! I'm sorry about that.

B Is there a bigger pool somewhere else?

A Um, let me think. Well, there's a big pool out of town.

B How far away is it?

A Maybe 20 minutes by taxi?

B That's fine.

A Just one thing. It's an outdoor pool.

B No problem. It's warm today.

2. **A** Hello there! How was the park?

B It was OK, but we were a little scared.

A Really?

B Yes. There were some young people there. They weren't very nice.

A Oh, I'm sorry to hear that. There's another park, but it's a 20 minute walk from here.

B That's OK. Actually, we want to see a movie now. Is there a movie theater near here?

A Not really. But there are many downtown.

B Oh, that's a little far. We walked too much today!

3. **A** Hello again! How was it?

B Market Street was perfect!

A Good!

B I have another question. I need to check my e-mail. Is there an Internet cafe around here?

A Well, there's a business center at the train station across the road.

B Is it expensive?

A To use a computer at the center? I think it's $5 for half an hour.

B That's $10 an hour. I guess an Internet cafe is cheaper than that, right?

A Right.

B Is there one near here?

A Not really. But there's a convenience store down the street. I think they have a computer there.

B That's great. Thank you.

A You're welcome.

4. **A** Hi! How was Cafe Centro?

B Wonderful. Really good.

A Excellent!

B I have one more question.

A Uh-huh.

B Is there a bookstore near here?

A No, sorry. But there are a lot of bookstores downtown.

B I see. How much is a taxi ride downtown?

A About $8.

B Eight dollars? That's good.

A Do you want to call a taxi?

B Actually, no. I have enough books. Thanks, anyway.

A You're welcome.

Unit 11

Listening . . . . p. 73

1. **A** Hey Carl, how was your vacation in Hong Kong?

B Terrible.

A Terrible? Why? Didn't you like Hong Kong?

B I loved Hong Kong. It's great.

A Then why was your vacation terrible?

B I broke my arm!

A Oh, no!

B Yeah. Actually, it was totally my fault, too. I just tripped over a rock.

A That's too bad.

Audio Scripts

B But I was lucky. I met a guy from England. He lives there, and he took me to see a doctor friend of his.

A That's great, but I'm sorry you had a bad time.

B It's OK, but I really loved Hong Kong. The people were great.

2. **A** Hi Ellen. Did you have a good time in Rome?

B Not at first! My plane was late, and the airline lost my luggage.

A What?

B My plane was late, and the airline lost my luggage!

A Oh, no!

B It was OK, though. The airline was really sorry about it, and they put me in a great hotel—for free!

A That's nice!

B Yes, and I met these really nice girls from Thailand. We went shopping in all these great stores.

A So you liked Rome?

B Yes. I loved the stores!

3. **A** Hi Brian, how was Acapulco?

B It was great… Well OK, I was on the beach, right, and I met these really cool people from Spain.

A OK.

B So we went out to have dinner. The food was absolutely amazing, and I got to practice my Spanish the whole time.

A Great.

B Yeah, but then something happened.

A What?

B I lost my passport.

A No! How did you do that?

B It was in my bag, and I left my bag on the beach.

A Oh, man! That's not good!

Listening Plus . . . . p. 73

A So, what did you do, Brian?

B First, I went to the Acapulco police, and I filled out a form.

A Then what?

B I said, "What about my passport? They said, "Sorry! Go to Mexico City." So I went to Mexico City.

A What happened there?

B I went to the Canadian consulate. They were really helpful. I filled out another form, and I made a list of stuff in my bag—my passport, a book, a pair of sunglasses, some sun cream… And then, something amazing happened.

A What? Tell me!

B I was still at the consulate, and guess what? I got a call from my hotel in Acapulco.

A Your hotel? Why?

B Because they found my passport under the bed!

A No!

B Wait, there's more. Then I got a call from the Acapulco police. They found my bag!

A Excellent!

B But they were really worried. This really nice woman said, "Sorry, señor, but there is no passport in the bag."

A Did you tell her?

B Of course. I said, "I'm so sorry, the passport was under the bed in my hotel room."

A So what did you do?

B I flew back to Acapulco, got my passport from the hotel, got my bag from the police, and enjoyed the rest of my vacation.

A Nice!

Unit 12

Listening . . . . p. 79

Presenter Hello and welcome to the Travel Show! Traveling is good for you—you can learn a lot when you travel, and, of course, it's fun. But traveling isn't always good for the environment. So the question is—can you travel and also help the environment? How can you be a green traveler? I talked to three young people, and I asked them: where are you going to go on your next vacation? Are you a green traveler? This is what they said.

1. Hi, my name is Steve Cassady. I usually take my vacation on a beach in Hawaii, and I take a plane to get there. This year, I'm going to Las Vegas, but I'm not going to fly there. I'm going to travel by motorcycle. Motorcycles use less gas, so they're a green way to travel. Also, they're very cool. The trip is going to take me two days, but I don't mind, because I love riding my motorcycle!

2. Hello, I'm Jennifer Morton, and I live with my family in New Jersey. My mom, dad, and my two sisters and I always take our vacation in the Appalachian Mountains. We usually take our minivan. This year, we're going to Florida, and we're not going to drive there, we're going to take the train. Actually, we're going to take three trains and a bus! There isn't a direct train route from here to Florida. My dad isn't happy about this, but my mom, my sisters, and I want to be green travelers, and we're very happy. It's going to be a long trip so I'm going to take a lot of books!

3. Hello, my name is Hank Stevens. I usually go to New York for my vacation, and I usually take a bus to get there. This year, I'm going to do something different. I'm going to visit Europe for the first time. I wanted to be a green traveler and not fly, but it's too difficult. There's a boat

121

Audio Scripts

from New York to England, but it's really expensive, much more expensive than the plane. So I'm going to fly. I'm not happy, I wanted to be green, but oh well…

Listening Plus . . . . p. 79

Presenter   Hello and welcome back to the Travel Show. Last week, I talked to Steve Cassady, Jennifer Morton, and Hank Stevens about their travel plans. Are they going to be green travelers? Let's find out.

1. Hi, Steve Cassady here. Well, this is it! I'm ready to go. It's about a thousand miles from here to Las Vegas, and I'm going to try to do half of it today. I'm not going to go sightseeing, but I'm going to stop to eat something, of course. Then I'm going to stay the night at a motel. On Day 2, I plan to go all the way to Las Vegas. Wish me luck!

2. Hi there, this is Jennifer. Well, we're on the train, and it's fantastic. We're going to arrive in Washington, D.C. in about an hour, and then we have six hours before our next train, so we're going to do some sightseeing. I'm really excited about it. This is my first time in D.C.! The next train is at 10 p.m., and we're going to sleep on it. I'm not sure about that but, hey, it's all good!

3. Hello, this is Hank, and I'm at New York's JFK airport. I'm in the departure lounge, but I'm not leaving any time soon. My plane is going to be at least four hours late. I don't mind sitting here. I have my laptop, and I'm writing e-mails and stuff. But the plane is very late, and I'm going to arrive in London late at night. I'm not very happy about that.

Unit 1

The verb *be*: statements and questions with contractions

We use the simple present of *be* to talk about a person's name, nationality, age, and job.
- *Are* you Sally?
- I *am* 20 years old.
- He *is* a doctor.
- My teacher *is* from England.

We often contract, or shorten, the verb *be*.
- I*'m* a student.
- He*'s* a teacher.
- I*'m not* a teacher.
- She *isn't* a teacher.

Affirmative statements		
I	am / 'm	
You / We / They	are / 're	from China.
He / She / It	is / 's	

Negative statements		
I	am not / 'm not	
You / We / They	are not / aren't / 're not	from Mexico.
He / She / It	is not / isn't / 's not	

We only contract *be* in negative short answers.
- No, I*'m* not.
- No, we*'re* not.
- ~~Yes, I*'m*.~~
- ~~Yes, we*'re*.~~

Yes/No questions		
Are	you / we / they	from China?
Is	he / she	

Short answers	
Yes, I **am**.	No, I**'m** not.
Yes, we **are**.	No, we **aren't**./No, we**'re** not.
Yes, they **are**.	No, they **aren't**./No, they**'re** not.
Yes, he **is**.	No, he **isn't**./No, he**'s** not.
Yes, she **is**.	No, she **isn't**./No, she**'s** not.
Yes, it **is**.	No, it **isn't**./No, it**'s** not.

Now Practice!

1 Complete the sentences with a contraction of *am*, *is*, or *are*. Check (✓) the sentences that are true for you and correct the others.

1. My mother _'s_ a teacher. ☐ <u>My mother isn't a teacher.</u>
2. I ____ 20 years old. ☐ _____
3. My birthday ____ today. ☐ _____
4. My dad ____ tall. ☐ _____
5. We ____ actors. ☐ _____

2 Answer the questions with information about you. Use contractions.

1. Are you a student?   <u>   Yes, I am.   </u>
2. Is your teacher from England?   _____
3. Are your parents doctors?   _____

123

Grammar

Unit 2

The simple present: affirmative and negative statements

We use the simple present for facts, routines, and states.
- *I live in Mexico City.* (fact)
- *We go to school on Monday.* (routine)
- *She feels tired.* (state)

We add –s or –es to the verb when we answer about a third person subject (*he*, *she*, *it*).

Affirmative statements		
I You We They	work live	in Tokyo.
He She It	works lives	in Tokyo.

Spelling rules: 3rd person singular	
Some verbs end in *ch, sh, x,* or *ss*. Add –es to these verbs. teach + es teaches wash + es washes fix + es fixes miss + es misses	Some verbs end in consonant + –y. Change the –y to –i and add –es. study -y + ies studies try -y + ies tries
These verbs have a special form: do → does go → goes have → has	

We use the helping verb *do* or *does* + *not* in negative statements. We usually use the contractions *don't* and *doesn't*.

Negative statements		
I You We They	do not work don't work	in an office.
He She It	does not work doesn't work	in an office.

Now Practice!

1 Complete the sentences and make affirmative statements. Use the verb in parentheses.

1. My sister __goes__ to a good university. (go)
2. My teacher _____ her job. (like)
3. I think a pilot _____ an interesting job. (have)
4. Most taxi drivers _____ in cities. (work)
5. My brother _____ a lot of TV. (watch)
6. A good student _____ every evening. (study)
7. My friends and I _____ good music. (like)
8. My brother _____ far away. (live) He _____ home. (miss)

2 Complete the sentences and make negative statements. Use the verb in parentheses.

1. My brother __doesn't have__ a job. (have)
2. I _____ near our school. (live)
3. My doctor _____ my name. (know)
4. My English teacher _____ French. (speak)

Grammar

Unit 3

The simple present: questions with *do*

When we ask *yes/no* questions, we use the helping verb *do* or *does*. It comes **before** the subject.
When we answer *yes/no* questions, we usually use contracted forms in negative short answers.

Yes/No questions				Short answers	
Do	you we they	**like**	pizza?	Yes, I **do**. Yes, we **do**. Yes, they **do**.	No, I **do not**./No, I **don't**. No, we **do not**./No, we **don't**. No, they **do not**./No, they **don't**.
Does	he she it	**like**	pizza?	Yes, he **does**. Yes, she **does**. Yes, it **does**.	No, he **does not**./No, he **doesn't**. No, she **does not**./No, she **doesn't**. No, it **does not**./No, it **doesn't**.

When we ask *wh-* questions, we also use the helping verb *do* or *does*. It comes **before** the subject and **after** the *wh-* word.

Wh- questions							
What	**do**	you we they	**like?**	What	**does**	he she it	**like?**

Now Practice!

1 Complete the questions with *Do* or *Does*. Then answer the question with information about you.

1. __Do__ you like sushi?   __Yes, I do.__
2. _____ most children like spicy food?   _____
3. _____ your school serve food?   _____
4. _____ your friends like French fries?   _____
5. _____ you work in a restaurant?   _____
6. _____ your father drink coffee?   _____

2 Complete the questions. Use the verbs in the box.

1. Where __does__ your teacher __live__?
2. What kinds of food _____ your favorite restaurant _____?
3. What kinds of food _____ you _____ in the morning?
4. Where _____ you _____ for pizza?

> go
> like
> live
> serve

125

Grammar

Unit 4

Frequency adverbs and word order

We use frequency adverbs to say *how often*.

Frequency adverbs	25%	50%	75%	100%
always	x	x	x	x
usually	x	x	x	
sometimes	x	x		
never				

Frequency adverbs usually go **before** the verb.
- We **always** exercise on Monday.
- She **usually** goes to the gym.
- I **sometimes** play tennis.
- I **never** go jogging.

However, with the verb *be*, frequency adverbs usually go **after** the verb.
- They are **always** hungry.
- He's **usually** on time.
- I'm **sometimes** late.
- She's **never** tired.

Sometimes and *usually* can go at the beginning or end of a sentence.
- **Sometimes** I play soccer.
- I go to the gym **usually**.
- The weather is nice **sometimes**.
- **Usually** he's late.

We don't use *never* with a negative verb. (*never* = not at any time)
- He's **never** late.
- I **never** go there.
- ~~She's not **never** tired.~~
- ~~I don't **never** go there.~~

We use *ever* in negative statements and questions. (*ever* = at any time)
- She isn't **ever** tired.
- Do you **ever** go there?

Now Practice!

1 Complete the sentences. Put the frequency adverb in parentheses in the correct place.

1. I'm hungry in the morning. (usually)
   <u>I'm usually hungry in the morning.</u>

2. I go to school on Saturday. (sometimes)
   _____

3. I exercise on the weekend. (always)
   _____

4. I'm happy. (always)
   _____

5. I go out with my friends on Saturday. (usually)
   _____

6. I don't eat a big breakfast. (never, ever)
   _____

Grammar

Unit 5

The present continuous: statements and *wh-* questions

We use the present continuous to show that something is happening now or for a limited time.
- *He's talking on the phone.* (It's happening now.)
- *I'm living in Tokyo now.* (It's for a limited time.)

We form the present continuous with the helping verb *be* + *–ing* form of a verb.

Affirmative statements			
I	am / 'm	reading	a book.
You / We / They	are / 're	reading	a book.
He / She / It	is / 's	reading	a book.

Negative statements			
I	am not / 'm not	watching	TV.
You / We / They	are not / aren't / 're not	watching	TV.
He / She / It	is not / isn't / 's not	watching	TV.

Wh- questions			
What	are	you / we / they	doing?
What	is	he / she / it	doing?

Spelling rules: *-ing* form		
work	+ *ing*	working
do	+ *ing*	doing
study	+ *ing*	studying
read	+ *ing*	reading
care	-e + *ing*	caring
dance	-e + *ing*	dancing
swim	double consonant + *ing*	swimming
stop	double consonant + *ing*	stopping

Now Practice!

1 Write the *–ing* form of these verbs.

1. write   <u> writing </u>
2. send   _____
3. sit   _____
4. have   _____
5. play   _____
6. take   _____
7. run   _____
8. exercise   _____

2 Complete the questions. Use the present continuous and the verb in parentheses.

1. What <u> are </u> you <u> doing </u> now? (do)
2. Where _____ your sister _____ now? (live)
3. What kind of music _____ your friends _____ to these days? (listen)
4. Who _____ your brother _____ to? (talk)
5. What _____ you _____ in school? (study)
6. What _____ she _____ for lunch? (make)

127

Grammar

Unit 6

The verb *be*: simple past statements

The verb *be* has two forms in the past: *was* and *were*.

- *I **was** late yesterday.*
- *My parents **were** at home last night.*

Affirmative statements					
I He She It	**was**	sick yesterday.	We You They	**were**	sick yesterday.

We usually use contractions in negative statements.

- *My teacher **wasn't** sick yesterday.*
- *My friends **weren't** at school yesterday.*

Negative statements					
I He She It	**was not** **wasn't**	at work.	We You They	**were not** **weren't**	at work.

Now Practice!

1 **Complete the sentences. Use *was* or *were*.**

1. Last night my friends and I ___were___ at the mall.
2. The stores _____ open until midnight.
3. My favorite store _____ very crowded.
4. It _____ really noisy everywhere in the mall.
5. By midnight I _____ very tired.

2 **Complete the sentences. Use *wasn't* or *weren't*.**

1. I __wasn't__ late to school yesterday.
2. The bus _____ crowded last night.
3. We _____ at school last night.
4. The weather _____ so bad yesterday.
5. It _____ very cold last weekend.

128

Grammar

Unit 7

Comparative adjectives: forms and spelling rules

We use a comparative adjective when we compare two people or things.
We often use *than* after the adjective.

- *I'm looking for a **cheaper** sweater.*
- *I'm **taller than** you.*
- *Old shoes are **more comfortable than** new shoes.*

We form comparative adjectives in 3 ways:

1. For most adjectives with one syllable, we add *–er*.

    sick → **sicker**
    small → **smaller**

    A few short adjectives have special spelling.

Spelling rules: short adjectives	
For short adjectives that end in *–e*, add *–r*.	*nice* → **nicer**
For short adjectives that end in one vowel and one consonant, double the consonant and add *–er*.	*big* → **bigger** *fat* → **fatter**
For short adjectives that end in *–y*, change the *–y* to *–i* and add *–er*.	*happy* → **happier** *lazy* → **lazier**

2. For most adjectives with two or more syllables, we use *more* + adjective.

    stylish → **more stylish**
    comfortable → **more comfortable**

3. A few adjectives have a special form.

    good → **better**
    bad → **worse**

Now Practice!

1 Write the comparative form of the adjectives.

1. big   _bigger_
2. hot   _____
3. baggy   _____
4. famous   _____

5. flat   _____
6. expensive   _____
7. dirty   _____
8. crowded   _____

9. interesting   _____
10. easy   _____
11. good   _____
12. beautiful   _____

2 Write sentences comparing the things in the parentheses. Choose adjectives from Activity 1.

1. _Tokyo is bigger than London._____ (Tokyo/London)
2. _____ (designer clothes/regular clothes)
3. _____ (English/Chinese)
4. _____ (coffee/tea)
5. _____ (a pilot's job/a doctor's job)

129

Grammar

Unit 8

Be like vs. look like

To ask about personality, we use *what + be + like*.

To answer, we use *be + personality adjectives*.

- What's Liz **like**?
- What's Paul **like**?

- She's smart and serious.
- He's funny and smart.

To ask about appearance we use:

1. *what + do + look like*

    To answer, we use *be + adjective* for appearance or *have + word* for physical features.

    - What **does** Ben **look like**?
    - What **does** Meg **look like**?

    - He's short and heavy.
    - She **has** blue eyes.

2. *who + do + look like*

    To answer, we use *look like + a person*.

    - Who **does** he **look like**?
    - Who **do** they **look like**?

    - He **looks like** Matt Damon.
    - They **look like** their father.

Be like: wh- questions			
What	**am**	I	**like**?
What	**are**	you we they	**like**?
What	**is**	he she it	**like**?

Look like: wh- questions			
What Who	**do**	I you we they	**look like**?
What Who	**does**	he she it	**look like**?

Now Practice!

1 Complete the conversations. Use *be like* or *look like*.

1. A What _____'s_____ your brother _____like_____?
    B He's funny and smart.

2. A Who _____does_____ he _____looks like_____—your mother or your father?
    B My father. He has my father's black hair.

3. A What _____are_____ your sisters _____look like_____
    B My older sister is very serious, and my younger sister is very shy.

4. A What _____does_____ your older sister _____look_____?
    B She's tall, and she has long blonde hair.

5. A What _____is_____ your favorite teacher _____like_____?
    B He's friendly and patient.

130

Grammar

Unit 9

Using *can* and *can't*

We use the helping verb *can*:

1. to talk about possibility
   - *We **can visit** the museum today. It's open.*

2. to talk about ability
   - *I **can't swim**.*
   - ***Can** you **speak** Spanish?*

3. to ask for and give permission
   - ***Can** I **come** in?*
   - *You **can go** home now.*

4. to make requests and offers
   - ***Can** I **have** a sandwich, please?*
   - ***Can** I **help** you?*

Affirmative statements

I You He She It We They	**can speak**	English.

Negative statements

I You He She It We They	**cannot speak** **can't speak**	French.

We usually use the contraction *can't* in negative short answers.

Yes / No questions

Can	I you he she it we they	**sing?**

Short answers

Yes, you **can.**	No, you **cannot.**/No, you **can't.**
Yes, I **can.**	No, I **cannot.**/No, I **can't.**
Yes, he **can.**	No, he **cannot.**/No, he **can't.**
Yes, she **can.**	No, she **cannot.**/No, she **can't.**
Yes, it **can.**	No, it **cannot.**/No, it **can't.**
Yes, we **can.**	No, we **cannot.**/No, we **can't.**
Yes, they **can.**	No, they **cannot.**/No, they **can't.**

Now Practice!

1 Complete the sentences with information about you. Use *can* or *can't* and a verb from the box.

1. I ____can't study____ in a noisy room.
2. I _____ a bathing suit to school.
3. I _____ Spanish.
4. I _____ a pizza.
5. I _____ tennis very well.

> make
> play
> speak
> study
> wear

2 Match the questions and answers.

1. Can I help you? _b_
2. Can I speak to Mr. Lee? ____
3. Can I have a coffee, please? ____
4. Can I look at your book? ____
5. Can you read this? ____

a. Sure. With milk?
b. Yes, I'm looking for Room 232.
c. Sure. It's on my desk.
d. I'm sorry, but he's not here right now.
e. No, sorry. I don't have my glasses.

131

Grammar

Unit 10

There is vs. *there are* and *some* vs. *any*

We use *there is/there are* to say that something exists (or doesn't exist).

- **There's** *a new restaurant in my neighborhood.*
- **There isn't** *one good store around here.*

We use *there is* with singular nouns, and *there are* with plural nouns.

- **There's** *a new movie at the theater.*
- **There are** *three new restaurants in town.*

Yes/No questions			
Is	**there**	a bank	in town?
Are	**there**	any banks	in town?

Short answers	
Yes, **there is.**	No, **there isn't.**
Yes, **there are.**	No, **there aren't.**

We often use *some* before plural nouns.

- *There are* **some** *good cafes in town.* (some = a few)

We often use *any* before plural nouns in negative statements and questions.

- *There aren't* **any** *movie theaters around here.*
- *Are there* **any** *shoe stores around here?*

Now Practice!

1 Complete the conversations.

1. A _____Is there_____ a good restaurant around here?

   B Sure. _____ one on the next block.

2. A _____ any noodles left?

   B No, _____. They were very good.

3. A _____ any convenience stores around here?

   B No, _____.

4. A _____ a shopping mall in this neighborhood?

   B Yes, _____. It's five minutes away.

2 Complete the sentences. Use *some* or *any*.

1. There are __some__ good stores around here.
2. There aren't _____ buses after midnight.
3. There are _____ beautiful parks in this city.
4. There aren't _____ mushrooms on my pizza.
5. There aren't _____ beaches near here.

Unit 11

The simple past: statements and questions

We use the simple past for completed actions in the past.
- Where **did** you **go** last week?
- **Did** you **go** by train?
- We **visited** Montreal.
- No, we **didn't**. We **drove**.

We add –ed for the simple past of regular verbs. For negative statements and questions, we use the helping verb *did*.

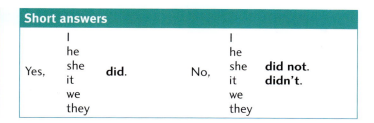

Affirmative statements	
I You He She **walked** to school. It We They	

Negative statements		
I You He She **did not** It **didn't** **walk** to school. We They		

Spelling rules: regular verbs		
visit	+ ed	visited
miss	+ ed	missed
talk	+ ed	talked
love	+ d	loved
hate	+ d	hated
study	-y + ied	studied
try	-y + ied	tried
stop	double consonant + ed	stopped

Yes/No questions	
Did you he she **stay?** it we they	

Short answers			
Yes,	I he she **did.** it we they	No,	I he she **did not.** it **didn't.** we they

Now Practice!

1 Write the simple past of the verbs.

1. play   _played_
2. wash   _____
3. know   _____
4. wear   _____
5. work   _____
6. forget   _____
7. help   _____
8. drop   _____
9. like   _____

2 Complete the sentences. Use the simple past.

1. I didn't go to the movies yesterday. I _went_ to the mall.
2. I _____ my luggage. I lost my wallet.
3. I didn't forget my passport. I _____ money.
4. She didn't break her arm. She _____ her leg.
5. I _____ a book. I bought a magazine.

Grammar

Unit 12

Be going to

We use *be going to*:

1. to talk about future plans

    - *I'm going to travel this weekend.*
    - *We're going to take a vacation next year.*

2. in predictions about the future

    - *Look at those dark clouds! It's going to rain.*
    - *We can't get there in five minutes. We're going to be late.*

Affirmative statements			
I	am 'm		
You We They	are 're	going to	study.
He She It	is 's		

Negative statements			
I	am not 'm not		
You We They	are not aren't 're not	going to	watch TV.
He She It	is not isn't 's not		

Yes / No questions			
Are	you we they	going to	study?
Is	he she it	going to	study?

Short answers	
Yes, I **am**.	No, I **am not**./No, I'm **not**.
Yes, we **are**.	No, we **are not**./No, we **aren't**.
Yes, they **are**.	No, they **are not**./No, they **aren't**.
Yes, he **is**.	No, he **is not**./No, he **isn't**.
Yes, she **is**.	No, she **is not**./No, she **isn't**.
Yes, it **is**.	No, it **is not**./No, it **isn't**.

Now Practice!

1 **Complete the sentences. Use *be going to* and the verb in parentheses.**

1. Cars ___are going to get___ safer in the future. (get)

2. Fewer people _____ by plane in the future. (travel)

3. More people _____ bicycles to work. (ride)

4. People _____ shorter vacations. (have)

5. I _____ around the world someday. (travel)

2 **Answer the questions with information about you. Use *be going to*.**

1. Are you going to take a vacation next year?
   Yes, I am. I'm going to visit my grandparents.

2. Are you going to study a language next year?
   _____

3. Are you going to try a new sport?
   _____

Vocabulary

Unit 1

Hey!
How are things?
How are you?
How's it going?

My name's _____.
Nice to meet you.
Nice to meet you, too.

How old are you?
What's your name?
Where are you from?
Who's that?

How about you?

fine
not bad
pretty good

brother
classmate
father
friend
mother
parents
sister
wife

actor
artist
doctor
photographer
student
teacher

Australia
Brazil
Canada
England
Germany
Ireland
Japan
Korea
Mexico
the US

Unit 2

actor
architect
chef
clerk
college student
doctor
model
office worker
pilot
police officer

producer
singer
soccer player
taxi driver
teacher
window washer
zookeeper

Unit 3

beans
beef
bread
cabbage
carrots
cheese
cheeseburger
chicken
chili pepper
dumpling
egg
fish
French fries
hamburger
home fries
ice cream
kebabs
lasagna
lettuce
meat
noodles
onions
pancake
pizza
potato
rice
salad
salmon
sandwich
seafood
shrimp
soda
soup
spaghetti
sushi
tea
tomato
tuna
vegetables

Chinese food
Italian food
Japanese food

breakfast
brunch
lunch
meal

Unit 4

basketball
bicycling
bowling
jogging
martial arts
skiing
soccer
swimming
tennis
weightlifting
yoga

do exercise
do martial arts
do yoga
exercise
go bicycling
go bowling
go jogging
go skiing
go swimming
go to the gym
keep fit
play basketball
play soccer
play tennis

Unit 5

check e-mail
cook spaghetti
do homework
have coffee
have lunch
listen to music
play a computer game
read a book
read a magazine
send a text message
study
study math
take a nap
talk on the phone
watch a game
watch a movie
watch TV

Unit 6

angry
awful
broken
busy
crowded
late
long
lost

panicking
sick
terrible

alarm clock
bicycle
bus
line
plane
station
suitcase
ticket
traffic
train
watch
weather

at a concert
at a party
at a soccer game
at home
at school
at the beach
at the mall
at work
in a hotel
in class
in the kitchen
in the mountains
on the phone
on vacation

at this time last week
at this time yesterday
last July
last night
last Saturday
last Saturday night
last week
last year
on December 31
on Friday
on Saturday night
on your last birthday
three months ago
today
yesterday

Vocabulary

Unit 7

designer clothes
dress
gloves
high heels
jacket
jeans
pants
regular clothes
scarf
school uniform
shirt
shoes
skirt
sneakers
suit
sweater
tie
T-shirt

baggy
black
blue
colorful
dark
new
nice
old
red
white

better
cheaper
cooler
more colorful
more comfortable
more expensive
more stylish
newer
nicer
worse

Unit 8

black/dark hair
blonde/red hair
curly/straight hair
long/short hair

good-looking
heavy
medium height
short
tall
thin

clean
confident
cool
friendly
funny
independent
lively
messy
neat
nice
patient
quiet
serious
shy
smart
sociable

man
woman

Unit 9

beach
building
cathedral
church
gallery
market
museum
palace
park
restaurant
ruins
statue
tower
zoo

fall
spring
summer
winter

Unit 10

bank
bookstore
cheap restaurant
coffee shop
convenience store
department store
gym
hotel
Internet cafe
movie theater
park
post office
restaurant
shoe store
shopping mall
swimming pool
train station

across from my house
across the street
around the corner
around here
down the street
in the neighborhood
in your town
near you
next door
on the next block
on Market Street
ten minutes away
two blocks away

Unit 11

break your arm
buy souvenirs
climb a mountain
fly
forget your passport
go shopping
go to a musical
go to a restaurant
go to a show
lose your luggage
meet someone interesting
miss your plane

sit on the beach
sleep in a hotel
stay home
stay in a hotel
visit a museum
visit an art gallery
write postcards

Unit 12

helicopter
limousine
motorcycle
plane
sports car
SUV
train
truck
van

drive a car
drive a truck
drive a van
go by boat
go by bus
go by car
go by plane
go by subway
go by taxi
go by train
on foot
ride a bicycle
ride a motorcycle
take a bus
take a taxi
take a train
take the subway

136

Mohammed Alsarab.
2025/3